HAUNTED
BERKSHIRE

Roger Long

The
History
Press

First published 2011

The History Press
The Mill, Brimscombe Port
Stroud, Gloucestershire, GL5 2QG
www.thehistorypress.co.uk

© Roger Long, 2011

British Library Cataloguing in Publication Data.
A catalogue record for this book is available from the British Library.

ISBN 978 0 7524 5907 3
Typesetting and origination by The History Press
Printed in Great Britain
Manufacturing Managed by Jellyfish Print Solutions Ltd

Contents

Author's Note

Having completed this, my nineteenth book, I thought I would start by answering a few questions that have been posed to me over the years.

- *Is there anything left of Berkshire?*

There certainly is. It is 50 miles of the M4, east to west, with an overlap of roughly 5 miles each side of the motorway. It stretches from John of Gaunt's Hungerford to the swarming, jam-packed Slough, renowned for John Betjeman's celebrated poem about the town ('Come friendly bombs and fall on Slough!'), and made famous by Ricky Gervais's popular television series *The Office*. Berkshire was presented with Slough some decades ago when Oxfordshire thieved the ghost-packed locations of Wantage, Wallingford, Abingdon, Faringdon and a plethora of villages.

- *Are there still any ghosts in such a small, modern and congested area?*

Certainly, but we are losing them by vast numbers. They are going as fast as our ancient inns. One constitution relies on the other, as eighty per cent of ghosts in England reside in pubs (poor overworked Dick Turpin appears in no less than sixty of them). What happens is a two-pronged assault; the pubs that close sentence their spirits to oblivion, while those that remain open are now smoke-free zones and, as we all know, spirits like to disappear in a cloud of smoke. If they cannot hide in the smoke leaving no trail, they are unlikely to appear in the first place.

- *Haven't you dealt with many of these ghosts before?*

No, but I have mentioned a sizeable percentage previously in some of my other books. However, as there has never been a book devoted exclusively to Berkshire ghosts, this offers a uniquely comprehensive a compact compilation for my ghost-hunting readers.

- *How are you different from other authors on the supernatural?*

For the simple reason; I visit and scrutinise every one of the sites I mention. In this I am unique. It is so simple to go to any good library, study a dozen books on ghosts and then classify and categorise them into book form, with chapters on seaside ghosts, theatre ghosts, haunted stately houses, rural ghosts, for example. I could go on forever. I once saw a TV programme where a 'supposed' ghost-hunter was apparently speaking to the ghost of a murderer in an ancient inn. He used the ghost's name to impress. What he did not know was that although the ghost was apparently real, the name was pure fiction, made up by a seventeenth-century writer. In another ghost book by a fairly well-known writer there is a supposedly true story where the author visits the scant remains of an ancient castle on the Surrey/Sussex border. He describes the atmosphere very well, so I thought I'd visit the place, but I could not find it. I paid three visits to the area and interviewed half a dozen local historians. I was finally taken to a field where all agreed the castle once stood. There was nothing there, not even a stone the size of a house brick. All who were present concurred that there had been absolutely nothing there since 1946. How our fearless ghost-hunter had walked between the ruined walls in the mid-1970s we shall never know.

- *Have you ever slept in a supposedly haunted room and have you seen a ghost?*

Yes I have slept in a haunted room on between sixty and seventy occasions, but as to whether I saw a ghost, I'm not telling.

- *Do you use any scientific equipment when seeking spirits?*

No, not usually. Occasionally I will use an optic.

- *Do you believe in ghosts?*

I think I'll be non-committal on that. I am a spirited agnostic, but I'll give you a quote from a very famous writer who, when asked the same question, replied, 'No, but I'm scared of them.'

For those readers following the trail, I have started my tour from the most westerly town, Hungerford, and then travelled east to Windsor calling at various towns upon the way. I have then headed south, taking in Wokingham, Sandhurst and more. At each town I have mentioned several villages that are easily accessible.

I should like to thank Brenda Allaway for the majority of illustrations and Dave Blackman for sorting out my haphazard report.

Roger Long, 2011

Also by the Author

A Grim Almanac of Old Berkshire
Curious Buckinghamshire
Curious Oxfordshire
Final Commitment: An Anthology of Murder in Old Berkshire
Historic Inns Along the River Thames

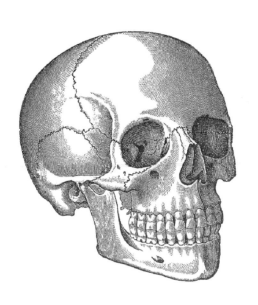

1

Hungerford

THE A338 at Hungerford is said to be haunted by the ghost of a lady on a white horse. She literally gallops across the road in broad daylight. This action has caused fist-waving motorists to swerve or brake suddenly. There is no information on who the spectral horsewoman might be, although it has been suggested that the lady may have been a local highwaywoman who is chasing a phantom coach and horses, which has been witnessed at the same spot. I find this unlikely though. The coach appears at night and as I've already stated, the lady appears in daylight. If she is indeed chasing the coach then she has got some catching up to do.

The Bear at Hungerford

Although the Bear public house appears to be an old coaching inn, it was adapted to become one. It was there hundreds of years prior to the coaching age. Here is a brief chronological history.

In 1298 there was some type of inn here, but it first came to notice in 1414. It is believed that it was named the Bear in reference to the bear baiting of the time. In 1509 it was owned by the Crown, in the person-

age of Henry VIII. In 1537 Robert Braybon, the landlord of the Bear, was instrumental in the capture of three highwaymen. Firstly, he heard them planning the robbery at Bagshot Heath when they were drinking in his inn. Secondly, he was able to send a potboy for the authorities when the three returned to the Bear to celebrate. In 1540 the Bear was partially rebuilt after a fire. The 1560s bore witness to several visits by Queen Elizabeth I. With respect, there are not many inns she didn't visit – also she reputedly haunts a good many of them. King Charles I assembled his troops at the Bear in October 1644. The year 1648 was a busy one for the Bear. William Bell, its most famous landlord, made his own tokens to spend at his inn. One of Bell's friends was the diarist Samuel Pepys, who spent many evenings at the Bear. Another visitor at that time was a highwayman, who hid in a barn and then attempted to rob the guests. In 1685 Mr Bell was in the news again when he sold a barrel of beer for eight shillings to the town constable to celebrate the defeat of Monmouth at Sedgemoor.

William of Orange arrived by coach in 1688 to do business with James II's advocates. The noise inside the inn was so vibrant that they had to do business in William's bedroom.

The Bear, Hungerford, a venue much favoured by spooks.

It was a waste of time; William spent the night with Thomas Dolman at Shaw House. When he awoke in the morning he was greeted with the news that James II had fled.

By the end of the seventeenth century, the Bear was a regular stop on the London-Bath-Bristol stage route and was owned by the Leybourne Pophams of Littlecote. In the early 1800s Sydney Smith, the famous preacher, journalist and wit played a joke on the owner. He booked a sumptuous feast for a Dean, an Archdeacon, a Canon, a Prebendary, a Rector, a vicar and a perpetual curate. The owner, chef and a multitude of lower orders waited for the splendorous diners who never showed up. Also in the 1800s there were several fires, one of which was said to be responsible for the death of two young girls. The girls who died are two potential candidates, out of a number, that might haunt the Bear. In 1821 people were sleeping three to a bed at the pub; the occasion was advertised as the greatest fight ever, a bare-knuckle contest of many rounds between Bill Neate of Bristol and Tom Hickman, known as The Gasman. Reports at the time estimated that 27,000 people converged in Hungerford in a single night.

On to the alleged ghosts. Firstly, there are two pairs of running footsteps that follow visitors down the stairs. These are suspected to be the two young girls that died in the fire. Incidentally, I have scoured many ancient papers of the time and can find no record of any deaths in fires at the Bear. This is not unusual; if people who died were not affluent or of suitable social standing, they did not get a mention. It was bad for the image of the town. Ironically, they were reported by newspapers in far away places, for example I have seen a Reading murder reported in detail in a Norwich newspaper, but it only occasioned two lines in the Reading press coverage. Also, I have seen lengthy accounts of a Stafford murder in a Reading paper. The Bear has a pungent aroma of cigar smoke, but when I used the Bear quite regularly it was pointless trying to investigate this as I smoke cigars continually. Also, I am informed that room eight, supposedly but doubtfully the room the young girls died in, has a mirror that refuses to be cleaned; a smudge always remains.

Great Shefford

The story of Wild Will Darrell of Littlecote has done more performances in the literary world than *The Mousetrap* has on stage. I personally have over thirty ghost books in which it appears – this will be the briefest one as yet.

Littlecote, now a sumptuous hotel on the Berkshire/Wiltshire border, was once the private abode of one Wild Will Darrell. In 1575, Mrs Barnes, a local midwife, was approached by two horsemen who blindfolded her and took her several miles away to a vast house. There her blindfold was removed and Mrs Barnes was taken into a large, beautifully furnished room. On a bed a masked lady lay in the final stages of childbirth; within minutes a baby was born. From a dark corner a tall man strode across the room gathered up the newborn baby and placed it on an open fire, holding it there with his boot until its life expired.

The dark figure was without doubt Wild Will Darrell. The lady, with very little doubt, was his sister Ada. In 1588, armed with a deathbed testimony from Mrs Barnes and a cutting taken from a curtain at Littlecote, Anthony Brooks, a lawyer, charged Darrell in court. Against all the evidence Wild Will was found not guilty. It seems a little strange that Sir John Popham, the Attorney General brought a good deal of influence on the case. Slightly before the charge Darrell had signed Littlecote over to Sir John on the understanding that he could live there until his death. It seems likely that this was a case of bribery.

In the event, Sir John did not have to wait long, in fact less than a year. Whilst riding

on Littlecote estate near Shefford Woodlands, Great Shefford, Darrell came to a stile, a feature very well known to him. As he started to dismount, a burning baby manifested and his horse reared, throwing him to the ground. Darrell smashed his head on the style and died instantly. And still, on some misty mornings the ghost of Wild Will rides through Shefford Woodlands. However I don't think the burning baby still puts in an appearance.

Lambourn

Lambourn is in fact a small town in its own right. In the late nineteenth century it was virtually dictated over by one man, Henry Hippisley, the bullying and defiant squire of Old Lambourn Place. Totally invulnerable to local feelings, Henry stripped the church of its cladding to use in repairs at Lambourn Place. No legal action was ever forthcoming; the villagers were left to seethe at their loss. Hippisley was taken to court for a type of misappropriation of funds for local almshouses, but he got away with an inept fine.

One of Henry's hobbies was to deflower local young girls, but a claim was made that one girl, who rejected his advances, died under suspicious circumstances. However, no body was ever discovered, even though

An illustration of Wild Will's horse accident, Shefford Woodlands.

I'm getting out of here hot-foot

frustrated villagers excavated large areas of Lambourn Woods. With no remains, there was apparently no crime and Henry was therefore exonerated. It is thought that he died of natural causes in 1890.

The ghost of Henry Hippisley was seen about old Lambourn Place for some years, although the building no longer stands. The ground has been built on and there has been no sign of Henry for decades.

Kintbury

In *The Haunted South*, Joan Forman relates several supernatural stories of Kintbury, including the romantically named 'Winding Wood Farm'. As the stories were brought to Joan directly from her correspondents it would be unfair to elaborate on them. However, the legends of Kintbury Church are well known in local folklore, therefore open to all.

The church houses the tomb of Mary Dexter, who wished to have her husband's sword buried alongside her. Approach the tomb at midnight and you will hear Mary's weapon banging against the stone of the tomb. Kintbury Church also has the shade of a man in a black cloak. He was noticed in the front pew one day; quiet chitter-chatter went on behind the stranger as the congregation wondered who he was and what his purpose was. Strangers stood out like sore thumbs in the tiny village and it was best to know their intent. Slowly the man arose and walked to the vestry. The congregation followed at a safe distance. When they had reached the vestry door the man in black had disappeared. There was no way out except by turning and passing through the crowd, all other exits were blocked.

The history of the twelfth-century church has just as strange a story. Once the bell tower was struck by a great bolt of lightning, ripping away the brickwork and tearing the great tenor bell from its housing. This was obviously the work of a witch. The good folk of Kintbury did not seek retribution; they merely sent the bell to be repaired. On its return the massive bell broke its fastenings and rolled into the River Kennet, coming to rest in the mud. The more the good folk tried to retrieve it the deeper it sank. The few that dithered before now knew without doubt that this was a witch's spell and so the advice of a cunning man or wizard was sought.

There is a poem about the actions that took place by Mr T. Major, but as it is long and the rhyming gets a little rasping, I shall try and set out the salient points. It was decided that two good women (old crones) would visit the cunning man and seek his advice. This they did, and his advice was to attach a bright new chain to the head of the bell. Then twelve white heifers, each led by a maid attired with a blood-red sash, should be attached to the chain. Each maiden was to carry a whip with a silvery thong to encourage the heifers. The job was to be done at midnight, on or about the time of a full moon; no one was to speak, sneeze or groan. The operation was to take place in absolute silence. All went well until a voice shouted, 'Here again comes the Kintbury bell in spite of all the demons in hell.'

At that moment the charm was broken and the terrible prediction took place; the chain snapped and the bell rolled back into the River Kennet, never to be seen again.

But who spoke those fateful words? Some over excited villager perhaps, or even the witch herself hiding in the crowd. Whoever it was, it was too late. The massive bell was never seen or heard again. That might not be quite true because they say that when the church bells are in full peal they are sometimes joined by a melodic sound coming from the depths of the River Kennet.

Kintbury Church.

Somewhere in the depths of the river lay the church bells.

I absolutely loathe being a cynic, but the Kennet has not quite the dimensions of the Mississippi or Amazon. When there has been a spell of dry weather it would be very difficult to misplace a bicycle bell in its depths, let alone a church bell.

Mildenhall

This is one of my favourite hauntings, even if I've had to take just a step or two over the Wiltshire border.

The story begins in 1879 when a carrier and his lad were taking a load of coal over Rectory Hill. On the descent both master and boy were walking at the horses head. Something unknown panicked the horses and they charged downhill at a horrendous rate, sending carrier and lad flying. Unfortunately the back wheels of the heavily laden cart went over the lad, Alfred (Alfie) Watts, crushing virtually every bone in his body. Poor Alfie died within two hours of his horrific experience. There was a small cross dedicated to Alfie Watts, aged 14, erected on the road between Mildenhall, where he died, and Axford, where he lived. However, the cross was never tended to and soon became overgrown by bushes and nettles.

In 1956, seventy-seven years after Alfie's demise, a party of four were travelling the road after leaving the cinema at Marlborough. As they approached the cutting at Rectory Hill the headlights illuminated a tall, thin, clean-shaven man standing before them. He was attired in a long white cloak or Mac. At a distance of 50 yards the driver sounded his horn. The man took no notice and the car drove through him; the occupants felt nothing. As they got out of the car to investigate the man disappeared. Although they realised that the steep inclines made it impossible for the figure to escape, they searched the banks for some time. Having accomplished nothing after ten minutes they proceeded home.

Having related the strange story to his mother, the driver was surprised to hear that he had experienced a run in with Henry Pound Watts, the father of the dead boy. Although he had died in 1907, the description fitted perfectly. As a girl his mother had met Mr Watts, who was easily recognizable by his long coat and his clean-shaven face, most unusual for the time.

There was no particular reason why Mr Watts's shade should appear at that time. However, the local council had recently decided to widen the road. When its programme manifested some months later, the small cross was dug up and thrown with other waste at the end of the cutting.

Over a year later some descendants of the Watts family were travelling along the specific road, in all probability to visit the small memorial, when they found it missing. They straightaway had it replaced very near its original setting.

Why did the ghost of Henry Pounds Watts appear? Can ghosts see into the future? Did he know of the authority's plans and intend the four cinema goers to remove the cross and replace it? Perhaps this is a bit far-fetched. They say that the cross remains there today; a few months ago I searched for it, admittedly briefly, but could not find it. I shall try again.

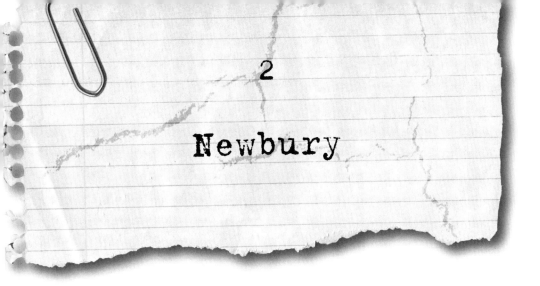

2

Newbury

I have always been a little disappointed in Newbury where ghosts are concerned. I have asked in several of the old central pubs, but am always answered in the negative. Landlords either deny the existence of ghosts, because they are too busy, or embroider and exaggerate the tales, hoping it will bring in trade.

One well-known ghost is that of Lord Falkland, who fell at the first Battle of Newbury (1643) during the Civil War. In those days the commanders were obliged to be at the centre of the fighting. Lord Falkland, Secretary of State, got entangled in a hedge with his horse and was literally slaughtered. His body was carried to a local farm. His ghost, complete with horse, has been seen quite regularly, although not recently. Perhaps the greatly increased traffic flow in the vicinity has chased the good Lord away.

Still regarding the Civil War, the Parliamentarian forces were holding the town in 1643. A witch was noticed sailing on a plank along the River Kennet and was seized by the forces. Some reports say that she escaped through sorcery but was recaptured and sentenced to be shot. Two men known for their marksmanship were selected for the

execution, but even from point blank range the witch caught the bullets in her teeth and more bullets bounced off of her. The soldiers then tried to slay her with a sword. Still no effect – it bounced off of her bony shoulder. Little did they know that the only rumoured way you could kill a witch is to shoot a bullet into the brain through an ear. However, one young trooper had heard the old tale about a witch's vulnerability and as he stepped forward the old hag began to cry and beg, but it was too late. The young soldier blasted her through the ear and she lay motionless.

But if you are strolling along the Kennet tow-path and you hear a light movement on the water, take care; it could be the old crone

Newbury's famous witch on a plank.

standing on a plank with her besom broom acting as a paddle. She is said to be quite a gruesome sight because now, apparently, her brains are hanging down her face and shoulder.

I believe every word of the tale.

Combe/Inkpen

Combe Manor was once a priory, but was better known as a rendezvous point for Charles II and Nell Gwynne. The summer-house, made famous by the Royal romance, still remains in what became Manor Farm. In the garden, figures in crinoline attire have been sighted and the mournful chanting of nuns has been discerned. And in living memory a small skeleton was discovered under a stairway.

The Crown and Garter pub at Inkpen is over 400 years old; a narrow lane running alongside the inn was once the main road to Salisbury. In 1676, this hospitable inn had an over-friendly (with the men) barmaid. She was Dorothy Newman, an attractive young widow. Dorothy realised her looks would not last forever and so she set her cap at George Broomham. George was honest, hard working and married; though he was besotted by Dorothy. George was putty in the young widow's hands. As they sneaked off to her bedroom, Dorothy described a simple plan that would involve them living together forever – only they would have to get rid of Martha, George's wife, first. Devoted, stubby, little Martha brought George his lunchtime meal each day. Near the top of the hill where George was presently working was a small pond surrounded by trees. How simple it would be to cudgel the young wife over the head and then drown her. It would be blamed on some itinerate tramp; there would be no problems for the lovers.

So it came to pass that several days later the plan was put into action. As Martha came with his food George sprang from behind a tree and cudgelled her to death. The pair then dragged the body to the pool and pushed it in. As they turned from a job well done, two small eyes were watching them, the eyes of George's small son Robert, who had followed his mother up the hill. Dorothy, acting in a split second, grabbed the boy and thrust his writhing young head and body under the water until he lay still. Unfortunately for the lovers, little Robert was not the only witness that fateful day. Dorothy's two boys had followed her on the unaccustomed journey. Shocked and horrified they fled back to the village, described the horrific scene and raised attention. A mob was sent to the hills and the couple were arrested. George was a broken man; the shock of seeing his son murdered was too much for him. He cleared his conscience and admitted all. The couple were convicted at Winchester and sentenced to hang at Combe Hill on a specially erected gallows. It had long been a bone of contention whether Combe was in Hampshire or Berkshire. Hampshire had no wish for a hanging; Berkshire had more stomach and accepted the commission as long as Combe was to remain forever in Berkshire, and so it was agreed. After days swinging on Combe gibbet as a warning, the bodies were brought down and laid in a barn at the Crown and Garter – a smell not conducive with dining one would have thought. While the couple lay in the barn there were tales of a low masculine crying. It was adjudged to be the spirit of George Broomham, weeping for his son.

Enborne

The trouble with the Newbury area is that most of the supernatural visitors go back

The Crown and Garter, Inkpen, where a deadly plan was conceived.

The famous gibbet in Combe.

to the Civil War era. If spirits are about for nearly 350 years they are pretty intrepid, they don't give up the ghost (so to speak) too easily.

During the battles of Newbury, Enborne was right in the thick of it. There are several places here where mounds are attributed to the many dead from the affair and there have been stories of shadowy figures. Whether it is the same shade that appears many times or various different ghosts is open to conjecture. Cope Hall is one of the favourite sites for the appearances; it was also the site of the murder at a far later date, so once again it is all conjecture.

Biggs Cottage at Enborne is thought to be haunted by the Earl of Essex. The Parliamentary commander stayed here the night before battle and two sisters living here reported his on his appearance – a smiling, jovial man, tall with a shovel shaped hat and a mode of attire suited to the mid-seventeenth century. I am always very sceptical of descriptions of spirits attached to their way of dress. Poor old Dick Turpin's ghost is doomed to haunt well over sixty pubs, well somebody in a tricorn hat is anyway. I have even interviewed a gentleman who thought his house was haunted by Laurel and Hardy because he had heard noises and then discovered two bowler hats in his attic.

Hoe Benham

Hoe Benham is a tiny hamlet just north of the A4, midway between Newbury and Hungerford. The story of Clarissa's Pig so intrigued me that I wrote a complete book under that name. Here is a précis of my original story.

In 1907 two young artists from London, Oswald Pittman and Reginald Waud had bought Laburnum Villa at Hoe Benham. The artists were new bohemians, parading the village in plimsolls, soft collared shirts and flowing locks of hair. The men were much appreciated by the local young ladies and any with a microcosm of artistic talent were invited back to Laburnum Villa.

One such young lady was Clarissa Miles, a keen if not highly talented local artist. On 2 November 1907, Pitman left his friend in the studio shed to purchase some milk from the milkman. As he glanced down the road, he noticed Clarissa approaching, accompanied by a long-snouted pig. On his return he informed Waud of Clarissa's companion and stated that he hoped she would leave her friend outside. On her arrival, a surprised Clarissa denied all knowledge of the pig and when Pittman pursued the point she insisted that the three of them walk back and discover what happened to it. This they did. Interviewing some children Clarissa had passed and the dairyman, both parties answered in the negative. The milkman added that he would be very much surprised if anybody would let their pig roam at will, especially as there was a swine order in the area and any straying livestock would be instantly destroyed.

Returning from Christmas in London, the two artists found Clarissa's story had become common gossip. The three were in a small way local celebrities, the toast of the Halfway House. Every local had a story; one old man informed the trio that once, as he and others returned on the hay wagon and passed King's Farm (Tommy King was a traditional ghost), the horses went crazy. What seemed to disturb them was a white blob bobbing about the horse's heads. They stayed in a frenzied condition well after the blob had floated into a nearby farm. Another farm boy had seen a floating pig-like beast and yet another had witnessed a sheep like creature. Being a brave man he struck at it with his crook, but the crook struck nothing solid until it hit the

The front cover of one of my books, which tells of some terrifying spectral animal spirits.

ground. A farming girl had heard uncanny squeals. Were they all in earnest or were the trio figures of fun?

It was possibly a mixture of both. As the trio walked down to the inn after Evensong one Sunday, Clarissa experienced a presence of vengeful evil and the physical sensation of having the life squeezed out of her. She was in a shaking, quivering, and almost incoherent state when she arrived at the inn. After she had steadied herself with a couple of drinks, she vowed that she would die at the inn rather than return past King's Farm. Several more drinks later and Clarissa was less adamant. She finally accepted that the only practical way back to Laburnum Villa was past the site

of the demolished King's Farm. As the three approached, a terrifying scream broke the night air. The intrepid trio fled to Laburnum Villa where they locked and barred the door. When the fear had subsided a little they realised that King Farm, the porcine spectre and the unearthly screams had taken place at exactly the same spot.

What else is there to say? The artists sold the house and Clarissa went back to whichever local village she came from. It is more than likely that the locals were joshing the newcomers. Let's face it; every crowd of local comedians had a mimic in its ranks, one capable of a terrifying horrific scream. Clarissa's pig and the various other blobby animals would be a lot more difficult. We shall never know, but we can look a little deeper into farmer King.

It is an unsubstantiated scenario based on scant facts: Tommy King was neither gregarious nor popular, just a lonely man, suspected rather than trusted by his neighbours. His farm was doing badly and he was probably depressed. We know he committed suicide by hanging himself from a beam in a barn. How long did he remain undiscovered? Days, weeks possibly. Who fed his motley brood of animals? Anyone? No one? Did they die of starvation? It's only a thought.

Thatcham

3

NICK Brazil tells us of several hauntings in Thatcham. One concerns a spirit child that was accepted by the family. Another set of manifestations appeared at Hartley Way and seemed to have behaved themselves, with only mild poltergeist activities. A third poltergeist briefly took up residence with a family at Pound Lane. They are all interesting accounts, but they are not my accounts, nor are they properties open to the public. So having mentioned them briefly I shall pass on.

There is, or was, an old manor house at Thatcham which I have been unable to identify. It was apparently the home of a ghost – unusual but not unique. But it was rare on account that it spoke. I only have notes on this and I'm not sure how I acquired them. But the shade was thought to inhabit the large larder.

'Moind moy poy!' was the three word sentence spoken by this ghost, which when translated from the Berkshire dialect means, 'Mind my pie!'

Another little ghost story, which I came across while researching *A Grim Almanac of Old Berkshire*: In 1930 an inquest was set up concerning the mummified remains of a baby found in the belfry of Thatcham Church.

When repairs were being made, a small box containing the even smaller cadaver was discovered in an air vent. The tiny body had been carefully wrapped in brown paper. At the inquest the pathologist suggested that there was evidence the baby had been strangled, either accidentally or on purpose. A local undertaker estimated that the wooden box was forty-five to fifty years old. The jury returned an open verdict.

It was then that the stories began to emerge that a cleaner claimed to have heard ghostly crying noises when she was at work near the belfry. A bell ringer related a similar story. Personally, I think more credence would be placed on these accounts had they surfaced prior to the tiny coffin's discovery.

Aldermarston

One would have thought that the old village lock-up would support a good ghost or two, but apparently not. It was used to make sure that the violent drunks did themselves or others no physical harm. There is one unauthenticated story that a drunk choked to death on his own vomit, but even he seems to have no inclination to return. There is also a

Somebody knew the identity of the mummified child's remains discovered in Thatcham Church.

Are the strange moanings heard in Aldermarston the pitiful death throes of a drunk who choked in Aldermarston lock-up?

story of a drunk in the lock-up who burned himself to death. There is a witch here well, to be more exact, the body of a witch. Maria Hale lies in the local graveyard, but her spirit will not rest and it is claimed that her ghost rises from the grave on damp winter nights. The logical answer is to place stones on her grave to stop her from rising up. It is a tradition for visitors to place an extra stone.

Two houses in Aldermaston have acted as the vicarage over the years. I believe they both still remain but no longer fulfil their original functions. Both are reported to be haunted. The first householder refuted the existence of a spirit and the second admits to having a Grey Lady. As both are now private dwellings please respect their privacy.

The Hinds Head pub in part goes back to the seventeenth century and it is thought that celebrations for the end of the Civil War were held here. Once named the Congreve Arms, after a respected local family, it acted as a lookout for local fires. If any were noticed, an alarm bell rang a warning from the tower. The alarm was sounded in 1845 when nearby Aldermaston Court was burnt to the ground. Also the drunk who was mentioned earlier is thought to walk the grounds, obviously disappointed that the Fire Brigades attempt to save him had failed.

The Butt Inn is a short way out of the village. In 1993 I asked the landlord if the old place was haunted.

'Oh yes,' he replied.

There followed a pregnant silence, it seemed he had no intention of elaborating.

'By whom?' I questioned casually; an approach I've often found to bring forth a response. 'A lady ghost, a gentleman, or what?' I persevered.

'Whatever it is, it turns on beer taps and slams doors,' he revealed. He would speak no further.

Bucklebury

For a small but widespread village Bucklebury is well supplied with ghosts. An evil spirit, rarely seen but often heard and smelt, chases unsuspecting people down Devils Steps. Slightly more often seen is a White Lady who flits over bushes and floats between trees in Oak Avenue, an attractive area planted on Queen Victoria's visit. A grisly apparition appears in broad daylight on common land called Bushnell's Green. More peaceable are the monks, varying in numbers that glide near the fishponds on the common, occasionally reported with fishing rods in their hands. Another strange force reputedly chases unwitting folk near Hawkridge.

A strange story comes from the Blade Bone Inn at Chapel Row. Outside the inn, and once acting as the signboard, is a large blade bone encased in copper. Villagers will relate the story of how their local heroes fought and slew a mighty monster or dragon. The blade bone has been kept as a souvenir and to prove the story. In fact it does the opposite. A consensus of expert opinion is that it is the bone of a dinosaur, probably found on the ancient common. However, the locals stick steadfastly to their more colourful story. As far as I know the Blade Bone Inn has no stories relating to the supernatural.

Probably the most famous of Bucklebury's ghosts is Lady Bolingbroke. Complete with her coach and four black horses she rides through the local roads on moonlit nights. Francis Winchcombe was married to the first Lord Bolingbroke, Henry St John. Royal impeachment sent Henry abroad in exile to France; his loving wife pined and then starved herself to death. As an expert horsewoman, her relief from loneliness was to race her carriage and four horses along the local roads.

It would be impossible and impolite to leave Bucklebury without mentioning

The fishponds on Bucklebury Common have their own eerie presence.

Cecelia Millson, a greatly appreciated writer and long-term resident of the village. I was slightly hesitant to include this story because it concerns ghosts that were not. Cecilia informs us that years ago people kept to their homes at night because they were terrified of a ghostly procession that walked the lanes. It consisted of four ghostly figures carrying a coffin. But one night, a courageous local man lay in wait for the spectral cortege. When it appeared, the man, complete with cudgel, jumped from hiding and beat the bearers mercilessly. They all fled dropping the coffin which, when opened, was found to contain a dead sheep, obviously stolen from a local farm. Similar tales are quite common in coastal regions where coffins usually contained contraband. This is the farthest north I have heard of such a caper and definitely the first one containing a sheep.

Stanford Dingley

There are three hauntings associated with this small village, although there is little known about any of them.

The best known is at the Old Boot Inn (local pub for Kate Middleton, Prince William's bride-to-be). It is the younger of Stanford Dingley's two pubs and one would have thought the least likely to be haunted, but in the nearby orchard a local man hanged himself. His spirit is reported to cause minor poltergeist disruptions at the inn. I have not called at the Old Boot of late, but in the late 1990s reports were getting less frequent.

Elsewhere in Stanford Dingley, the Old Rectory is a splendid Georgian house of mellow red brick. It has a wooden donic design door case and attractive dormer windows. It also has a ghost and there the description ends; locals seem to know little if anything more.

And finally, in this village yet another Grey Lady is reputed to haunt the area of Jennet's Wood at midnight.

The Old Boot Inn, Stanfold Dingley, where a suicide took place.

The Royal Oak, Yattendon, where you can hear some very creepy noises.

Yattendon

Yattendon is a very attractive village, surrounded by Christmas trees. I wonder how many lorry loads I took out of there as a teenager working with the local travellers. There is a wide street, which resembles a square here.

The strangely named 'Mrs It' haunted the old Rectory here for many years. She was described by the Rector's wife in the mid-1940s as being greyish-black looking like smoke and with a body of the same consistency. The lady was unusual in the way that she seemed always in a hurry. Logically speaking this is bizarre; why should a ghost be in a rush to get anywhere?

The busy lady wore what was described as a shawl over a watered silk dress. On her head was a bonnet of Victorian times and she carried a basket. The Rector's family of that time met the old lady on many occasions and found her charming. They also named her 'Mrs It'. However it is commonly believed that she was the unmarried sister of the Reverend Puller, who lived there in the 1720s. I have used the past tense in the above story because there has been a successful exorcism at the Rectory. Why, I don't know; old 'Mrs It' seemed very happy there and troubled nobody. Let us hope that she has not been condemned to ever lasting limbo.

There are still people in Yattendon who have experienced a meeting with the ghost Henry. Henry is a relic from the Civil War. When troops of either side were advancing and retiring through villages, they lived off of the land. They helped themselves to anything the farmers and peasants possessed; even rape was not unusual. Things could be more than a little scary if one was caught alone, especially if in the act of committing a crime like this. Henry, a parliamentarian trooper, was caught in such a situation. Calling for help was not an option, as the local peasants bound and gagged him before hanging him high from a barn beam. Henry is thought to haunt several lanes around the barn; he is dressed in his buttoned uniform tunic and floppy hat. It is disconcerting to any walker that comes across Henry by accident. It is even more alarming if you happen to be one of the numerous drivers who have driven through him over the years.

A well-known legend of Yattendon concerns the villagers during the Civil War. They were forced to flee from their homes, but before leaving they had hidden their combined treasures in a well that was surrounded by a field. It is unknown if, or when, the villagers returned but a guard they left was subsequently killed. Loyal to the death and even longer, his spectre still patrols the area guarding their fortune. Unfortunately, this particular well has never been traced, though many others in the vicinity have.

One well, situated under the Royal Oak, had tragic consequences. A Mrs Faithfull fell to her death when the floor of the inn opened up beneath her, sending her down the well shaft. There have been rumours of hauntings at the Royal Oak for many years, but they have nothing to do with the unfortunate lady. The strange rumblings, sighings and reverberations could have much to do with the passages and shafts beneath the inn. Apart from that, the supposed hauntings had been going on many years before Mrs Faithfull's sad demise. In fact the murmuring ceased when the well had been filled in with many tonnes of slate.

Leaving Yattendon towards Frilsham, I am told there are some haunted chalk caves; what or whom they are haunted by, I have not been informed, but still, I shall put them on my visiting list for the future.

4

Reading

READING is very barren country indeed for the ghost-hunter, and what is there is very difficult to pinpoint. I once heard about a schoolboy here who could levitate, and being a keen young reporter I did my best to trace him, but to no avail.

Just as difficult to track down is a four bedroomed house in Oxford Road. I have seen reports in which there are descriptions of an old lady ghost who is always accompanied by the strong aroma of flowers. A young family apparently lived there and the children were much alarmed. Try as I may I could not find the house. It's a little embarrassing knocking on every fourth door and enquiring, 'Have you an old lady ghost here who smells of flowers?'

I gave up after an hour; the house may well have been knocked down and the Oxford Road seems 20 miles long.

When we were children we used to cycle past Searle's Farm. The gaunt, somewhat menacing old building had to be haunted. I think we took turns to see who could make up the most menacing, terrifying, colourful and unlikely story. I am indebted to Nick Brazil's *A Journey with Ghosts* for a tale which is a little more likely.

A one-time driver informed the author that he had taken an overnight lodging at the old farm. The young man was visited in the night by the shade of a young lady in white flowing robes. The figure was described as self-illuminating. The driver was questioned suspiciously by his hosts the following morning. The family knew very well of their ghostly visitor and had placed the young man in that room as a type of test. After the driver had admitted seeing his spiritual visitor, his hosts went on to explain the strange lights in rooms and other supernatural occurrences. The lady in white is purported to be the shade of a young servant girl who, finding herself pregnant out of wedlock (an unpardonable sin in the 1800s), committed suicide from an upstairs window. Supposedly the haunted bedroom is the room she jumped from.

Nick Brazil goes on to inform us of a hidden room found at Searle's Farm. The tiny room, near a fireplace, was discovered during alterations. The cell concealed a small chair and table, suitable only for a midget or a child. Such hidden rooms or cells are fairly common; there are countless priest holes in ancient buildings all over the country. There is one, in one of my local pubs. Nick suggests that another possible purpose was that the room was some secret memorial to the tragic suicidal servant.

There is, however, at least one other possibility. For many decades, children who had not been christened were not permitted to be buried in hallowed ground, hence the rush to have sickly babies christened as soon as possible after birth. Many tiny bodies have been found entombed between walls of old houses. Some close friends of mine did some extension work to their ancient home, an old dairy in Glastonbury, and discovered a small box or coffin containing the skeleton of a baby; it was quite a shock. Local specialists could not tell whether or not the tiny cadaver had died of natural causes. I suppose it matters very little now.

One pub in Reading, the George, is a beautiful place that I have covered on several occasions. It is an old coaching inn, sitting sedately in the centre of Reading. I have not been there for some time, but for decades an old coach was placed in front of the hotel; I hope and trust it is still there. The passengers would alight here before the horses were stabled for the night in Kings Street or Minster Street. In a town like Reading, some 40 miles from the capital, and on the main route to Bath and Bristol, customers were spoilt for choice with comfortable inns to stay the night – the George needed to maintain its position as first choice. Reports stated that it was beautifully clean, colourfully decorated and famous for its lavender coloured sheets.

In 1812 Mr Moody, a large coach proprietor, ensured that his customers were entertained while spending the night in Reading. He provided funds to the landlord of the George to purchase two baskets of rotten eggs. While waiting for the horses, passengers liked nothing better than to take a short walk up to the Market Place. Once there they enjoyed themselves by pelting the occupants of the pillory and stocks. One passenger, writing in his diary, claimed he had had a splendid time. Apparently a local cook had supplied rotten meat and offal as extra ammunition. What is not usually appreciated is that the pillory, unlike the stocks, could be a death sentence. Unless the victim could afford to employ a man to wipe his face he could easily die of suffocation.

Enough of this scene setting, what about the ghost? Rather innocuous I'm afraid. There is a very cold patch on an upstairs landing and an old lady, thought to be an ex-servant, has been witnessed there. She just smiles and disappears.

The Roebuck is another interesting pub, situated on the western end of the Oxford Road (A329 towards Pangbourne). It's a large and not particularly attractive pub when viewed from the road; but there is more of a decent vista looking over the Thames at the rear. This was reputedly the home of a retired admiral; the shade of this gentleman is the resident ghost at The Roebuck. However, his name is unknown, which seems strange with the amount of data now available.

Also, it is rumoured that the retired naval officer met an untimely and suspicious death. This in turn is held responsible for the poltergeist activity. A former landlord claimed that locked doors and windows mysteriously opened, furniture moved and heavy footsteps were heard at night. Dogs even refused to go into certain rooms, one of which was where the legendary admiral would stand with the spyglass concentrated on the river. Some say he was expecting a French Armada to come up the river, having conquered London previously. Little has been heard of the admiral recently; perhaps we are now safe from the French fleet.

In the late 1990s The Roebuck was altered to a themed pub called The Beethoven. I was doing a programme for Radio Berkshire here

The George, Reading.

The Roebuck, Reading, home of the phantom admiral.

and in a foolish minute I announced that I had better go before I got Brahms and Liszt … Have you ever regretted saying something? My listeners, all 250,000 of them, didn't find it funny either.

Basildon/Lower Basildon

I have heard about supernatural happenings down at the Grotto for a number of years. The attractive building looks out over the Thames and has served a number of purposes since its erection in 1746. During the Second World War, the Grotto was a base for Land Army girls. Imaginations may have been coaxed a little, as is often the case when the young are in abundance, but there were several sightings of Lady Susanna Fane. I am indebted to Hilary Stainer Rice and her book *Ghosts of the Chilterns and Thames Valley*, for more detailed information.

Lady Fane, youngest daughter of John Marriott of Suffolk, lived at The Grotto until her death in 1792. Whoever or whatever haunts the old building is not known, but Hilary informs us that a plethora of secretaries left in quick succession when the building was run by the Institute of Leisure and Amenity Management during the 1960s to 1980s. All complained of seeing a white transparent lady passing them on a stairway. Two boys reported seeing Lady Fane near the site of an old tennis court. Described as a flimsy wraith, the spectre made its way towards the Thames.

Obviously, mysterious tales abound in such a place. One tells of a secret tunnel, another of a sealed room and a third of bells that are inclined to ring. Also, the means of Lady Fane's demise are varied and colourful. One has her falling into a well and drowning, a second has the time-honoured story of the mistletoe bough.

Basildon House, the Grotto.

The oft-told tale is of a lady that hid in a self-locking chest and died of suffocation. It has at least a dozen venues, Marwell, Minster Lovell and Bramshill Police College being three of the better-known contestants. In all probability, Lady Susanna Fane died an old widow.

Hilary goes on to inform us of the nearby old gardener's cottage where the lady occupant saw a door handle turn. Opening the door surreptitiously, she found no one on the other side. The same lady had trouble with an electric clock that fell to the ground, narrowly missing her. In yet another close abode strange footsteps are heard, a bedroom door opens itself at night and a disconnected bell rings.

Basildon Park, which was inherited and quickly sold in 1766 by Lady Fane and three others, has strange but unsubstantiated supernatural stories of its own. It also had an intricate octagonal well house. It is suggested that a servant might have drowned there, thereby giving rise to the fanciful story of Lady Susanna Fane's watery demise and subsequent spirit.

There are two other ghosts attached to Basildon, of which little or nothing is known. Nobes on his white horse, is thought to be a phantom hunter who frequents (very infrequently) the paths beside the A329. He was thought to have lived at Tomb Farm and to have died in a hunting accident.

The other, Nan Carey, is supposed to have been a witch who, after her demise, haunted a lane in the area. Absolutely nothing else is known.

Caversham

An old haunting in Caversham is related by the Honourable John Byng when he stayed with friends in 1781. Byng sat with the family in their gallery, an extremely atmospheric place. I am more than a little sceptical of one of the hauntings supposedly witnessed here. At midnight, a coach, complete with headless horses scours through the house. Supposedly it terrifies those that are awake but does not waken those already slumbering; very considerate of it.

A carpenter named Pullyen is thought to have been spook number two in the house. Pullyen committed suicide here, but how, we are not informed. What we are informed of is the strange and irregular hammerings that were sometimes heard. The exact location of the house in which Byng was a visitor is unknown. The chances of its remaining today are more than unlikely.

When I was researching my first book, *Murder in Old Berkshire*, I was delighted to unearth the murder of Jonathan Blagrave. In 1723 Blagrave, a wealthy, boastful, and boozy farmer, had done well at Reading Market. It took him some time to arrive home; he did not leave the Griffin until 3 o'clock in the morning. Being well in his cups and generous to a fault, he had openly boasted and showed the day's shrewdly gotten gains. Unfortunately for Jonathan, three youngsters, two young men and a young maid overheard him. They lay in wait for him where he was known to take a short cut alongside the river. Here he was attacked and his skull smashed. Jonathan made it to the Thameside Roebuck (no longer there) where he died a few minutes later. His donkey and cart remained by the river.

Could the occasional unsteady shade that has been witnessed on the Caversham towpath be Jonathan Blagrave, the jovial farmer? Could he be staggering from alcohol, a smashed skull or possibly both?

Englefield

Englefield House is a mighty Tudor mansion with towers and turrets equal to any fabrication of a Disney dream castle. When I had a job delivering in the area, I used to eat alfresco besides its tree-shaded drive. In such surroundings, it is not surprising that the ghost of a previous owner, Powlett-Wright, is said to haunt the house at night. Powlett-Wright was an adventurer who spent much of his time at sea. Whilst away on various voyages he left Englefield House in the hands his brother. Perhaps the brother became a little too fond of the luxurious way of life, for he firmly ensconced himself in the premises, simultaneously inventing a story that his brother had died at sea. There might just have been some truth in the story, as it is claimed that Powlett-Wright never visited the house in his human form again. A sailor's face at a window is said to have been his and the shade of the adventurer is said to visit the churchyard to inspect his wife's grave.

Farley Hill

Farley Hill was home to a pet witch who lived in a cottage besides the Reading Road in the eighteenth century. As we all know, witches are thought to be capable of turning themselves into black hares at the slightest whim. One day, some children saw a hare in the vicinity of the old witch's cottage and they chased it and pummelled it with stones. One stone was a direct hit on the hare's hind leg; crying with pain it hobbled its way into the witch's garden. The children in full cry followed at a pace but the hare was nowhere to be seen. One boy, the leader of the pack, pushed open the cottage door and, you've guessed it, the witch was on the floor writhing in agony with a nasty fresh wound upon her leg. The cottage is long gone, but on certain nights lonely walkers hear deep moaning coming from where the cottage once stood.

Padworth

Padworth, a very pleasant little village has some mysterious lights. Many years ago, farmers from the village walked their sheep and cattle along the lonely lane to Reading market. The animals are long gone, but the lanterns the farmers used reappear at intervals. Edward Hobbs, the Padworth Parish clerk from 1871 to 1911, sometimes saw the lights and worked out that they appeared at a specific time on particular nights. Hobbs described them as carriage lamps and said they moved quite quickly, a diagnosis at odds with the accepted shepherd's lanterns. When approached they disappeared, leaving the observer with a strange and eerie stillness. Some villagers insist that the lights remain and this has been verified quite regularly in living memory.

The witch who transformed herself into a hare at Farley Hill.

Caversham towpath, walked by the murdered Jonathan Blagrave.

Englefield House.

Englefield Church.

A towpath in Purley that some people find very disturbing.

Purley-on-Thames

It is some years since I last visited the Coach House at Purley on Thames and if it isn't haunted, I would be very surprised. Catch it in the early morning, with the mist rising from the river, and you will understand what I mean. I had heard about a secret chapel discovered here not so long ago, reputedly for the use of persecuted Catholic monks from Mapledurham House. I was pleased when Nick Brazil confirmed the fact in *A Journey with Ghosts*. Nick goes on to relate several strange stories of the Coach House, but as they are his stories and not mine I must satisfy myself with the better known, if brief, account of the headless horseman that supposedly haunts a patch of ground where stables once stood. That is word for word all I know of the story.

While mentioning Purley, Nick goes on to tell of a footpath, quite well known to me, where galloping footsteps have been heard. This may or may not be concerned with the Civil War siege near Caversham. Be that as it may, I have found that this particular bridleway has an air of depression attached to it. I nosed about here for some time while writing my *Historic Inns of the River Thames*. Also, apparently, the late Angus Macnaughten tells of a spiritual encounter here, related to him in turn by the editor of the *Reading Standard*. A casual observer might decide that there are more ghost-hunters than ghosts here.

Sonning

One would have thought that the many ancient buildings of one of Berkshire's most attractive villages would have been festooned with ghosts. I am still of the opinion that this is the case; I could however find very little, or perhaps people were very taciturn about

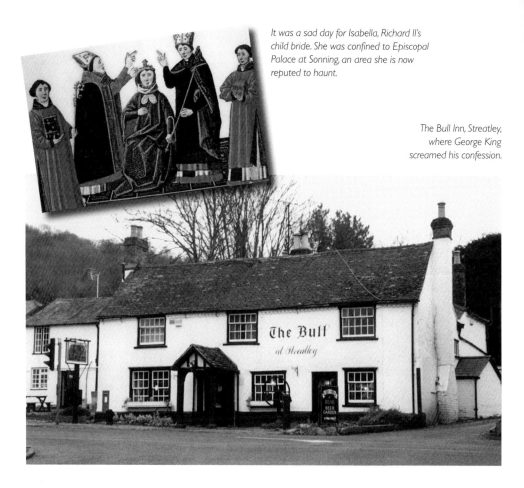

It was a sad day for Isabella, Richard II's child bride. She was confined to Episcopal Palace at Sonning, an area she is now reputed to haunt.

The Bull Inn, Streatley, where George King screamed his confession.

admitting to such enforced guests. We must be content with Isabella, a very ancient ghost indeed.

Here's a brief history lesson, which I have recently researched. Isabella was the daughter of Charles VI of France; she was the child bride of Richard II. After his murder at Pontefract Castle, Isabella found herself a prisoner of Henry IV in the Episcopal Palace at Sonning. Although Isabella spent a very sad time here, grieving Richard, she did not die here, as she returned to France in 1400.

It is rumoured that Richard survived the attempt on his life and escaped to Scotland, where he died in 1419. It is also speculated that she remained in communication with him for many years. All however is hearsay.

Whatever the circumstances they did not stop Isabella from marrying her cousin, the eldest son of the Duke of D'Orleans. She died following the birth of her first child in 1410.

Why is it then, that the weeping spectral woman that floats along the river bank and around the Episcopal Palace is assumed to be Isabella? It is believed to be so, by her gentle manner and her style of dress.

Streatley

The Bull Inn. There was once a nunnery here, in this most ancient of villages, between Goring Gap and the gliding Thames. It was from this nunnery that an errant nun made her way to the Bull for a clandestine meeting with a novice monk. The pair were caught and slain, probably in a most barbaric fashion. Two yew trees were planted over their graves and may still be seen today. Legend dictates that on the anniversary of their execution, two figures rise from the graves and walk into the mist.

The Bull Inn is on the A417 Reading to Wantage Road and is home to less well-known murders too. One such murder concerned George King, a young transient farm worker who slew his old landlady at her pub, the White Hart in Wantage, almost decapitating her with a beanhook. King was transported from Wantage to Reading, a long and very dry journey by cart. The Bull at Streatley was one of several stops the guards made for sustenance. On entering, King noticed a picture on the wall which very much resembled his victim, Ann Pullin. In his demented state King decided she had come to haunt him. He lunged at the picture screaming, 'I'll kill you again, I'll kill you again!'

The deranged farmhand was restrained and taken to Reading, where he was tried, convicted and hanged for his crime. It is interesting to note that when his body was handed to the surgeons (a common practice), it was found that King had a large tumour on the brain. His might have been a different story in more enlightened times.

Tidmarsh

Just down the road from the Greyhound is a small stream. This is the abode of the Moon Boy. He rises from the stream in which he drowned on clear moonlit nights. Two locals passing the Old Rectory on their way home from the Greyhound pub saw the back of a young naked boy manifesting himself. It was lucky for the locals he did not turn and stare at them with his terribly bloated face. Such an action foretells of a death in the observer's close family.

Tidmarsh, home of the Moon Boy, a drowned lad who appears on moonlit nights.

Probably the best-known private house haunting in Wargrave is Barrymore's. Please remember that this is a very private residence, but nearby Rachel's Well, a finely illustrated natural spring just down the road, is open to the public. Also, while here, a drink at the Horns is most satisfactory. There have often been tales of supernatural experiences near the inn but I could glean no more information.

Back to the Barrymore's. This was once the home of the wicked and idle Irishman, Earl Barrymore. His talent for spending money was reckless to the extreme. When he was in his cups, his escapades were notorious; he was once thought to be Springheeled Jack, but this was never the case. Among other feats were Barrymore's regular rides through the village, putting shots through inn signs and tipping over stalls and fruit barrels. Most of these actions were tolerated silently by the populace for they realised that, when sober, the young Earl would recompense them generously.

In 1782, he built a state-of-the-art theatre in the village. It was patronised by the high and mighty of the day, not the least of which was George IV. Barrymore bought himself a commission in the army, but he was not suited to its discipline. He died by accident in 1793 while escorting French prisoners at Dover. Reports of his death being suicide have very few facts to back them up.

Barrymore was only twenty-three at the time of his death and his only accomplishment was to have amounted debts of about £300,000. He was buried in Wargrave Church chancel with the ever present threat that creditors would take his body and hold it to ransom.

So does the wicked Earl haunt Barrymore? Strangely, no. The ghost is a fairly well substantiated Grey Lady who favours the staircase. Her pedigree and association with the house is unknown.

A White Lady, a breed only slightly less prolific than the Grey Lady, is said to haunt both her old home, Gaunt Cottage, and the property next door, Little Gaunt. Joan Forman, in *The Haunted South*, made enquiries and found that the former Gaunt Cottage is said to be haunted, while the occupier of Little Gaunt denied it emphatically.

Wargrave, small as it is, has an array of pubs to visit. The only inn on the High Street that doesn't seem to be haunted is the Greyhound. The Bull has been haunted for many years by the sound of a weeping woman in what is called the Tear Room, an upstairs bedroom that is reputed to have an extremely depressing atmosphere. The story goes back to the 1820s when the then-time landlord discovered his young wife with a lover and cast her out. Despite forbidding her to approach him, the inn or their young child again, the lady made several attempts to return and begged to see her baby; all her pleas were denied. After several years she died of a broken heart. It is the weeping and moaning of the errant wife as she packs her few belongings that is heard on the anniversary of her departure. The trouble is that no one knows what date that is.

The haunted story concerning the White Hart is tenuous indeed. The White Hart is a most attractive inn, internally as well as externally. It covers several centuries with its design. Slightly incongruous, but nevertheless almost unique, is an old petrol pump on the site.

What interests us is the sign; it depicts a white hart adorned by a lavish gold collar. The story goes that the King (we are not told which one) was enjoying the hunt in Windsor Forest. A particular white hart gave the King a long and adventurous chase through the woodland and along the riverside. They finally cornered the animal near Wargrave, but the appreciative King refused to permit the kill. Instead he placed a gold collar around the hart's neck so that it would be instantly recognized and not hunted by Royal decree.

For many years long after its death a phantom white hart was spotted on the hills above Wargrave. Call me a cynic and unromantic if you will, but I should have thought that bedecking a deer with a gold collar in a land of starving peasants would have assured its demise in a matter of hours. I wonder what became of the collar.

The next pub along the way is the George and Dragon. I have quite often related the story of this pub, though it is not so much to do with the pub, more concerning the ferry that ran very close to the inn.

On 25 January 1879, Colonel Markham of Shiplake House decided to take his young daughter skating on the Thames. After a while he tired of the sport and hailed the ferry. On the short trip to Shiplake the boat hit something, got trapped in the floating ice and sank. There were four people on board the tiny craft. The Colonel and ferryman made it to the bank and Miss Markham was pulled out at the George and Dragon by two courageous local men, Fisher and Wyatt.

Unfortunately the 10-year-old daughter of Essex Thomas, the ferryman, who had come along for the ride, was lost beneath the water. At the time much was made in the papers of the Markham's unfortunate accident. There was little or no reference to the drowned girl. It was only through the diligence of a local author that her name was ever known; Mary Anne Thomas.

There have been reports over the years that a small child's face is seen looking pleadingly up from the water. Personally I don't believe this to be Mary Anne Thomas. There had been reports of this particular shade long before this tragic accident.

The White Hart, Wargrave.

St George and Dragon, Wargrave.

There's more; on 5 July 1926 a young woman was pulled barely alive from the Thames at Wargrave. On revival her story was mysterious but not unique. The young lady had enjoyed an evening meal at the George and Dragon. Some 200 yards from the inn, on her return home, she heard an enchanting, captivating, melodious tune coming from the water. Looking down she saw a face, a mischievous but reassuring face that seemed to draw her towards it. The urge to join the young spirit was undeniable and strong, a sort of calling that could not be denied. Within seconds she was floundering in the water; she had been a victim of Benji or Binji, a child of unknown gender that attracts young people to a watery grave. The young lady was saved by two local boatmen. Perhaps she was lucky; there have been several seemingly unproved suicides near the spot.

It was nice to have a haunting surprise in Wargrave, in the form of a pair of stories unearthed by Joan Forman, concerning Gilbstroude Farm. The first concerns the daughter of the farmer, who seems to have preferred financial security to love. She jilted her young lover for the safety of an older man's arms. The ex-lover got some sort of revenge by painting the picture of a gruesome, malignant ancient man. Apparently he presented this to his ex and disappeared. One assumes that the picture was a warning for the future and perhaps a blight on the couple's happiness. The picture hung by the stairs for years, where, we are informed, the moonlight exaggerated the malevolence of the old man's expression. Finally it was placed in the barn where Joan was permitted an inspection.

Run that by me again please. Is there something I'm missing here? Why keep a picture that was wounding and offensive for years when the couple could have thrown it out or refused to accept it in the first place?

Joan also informs us of the ghost of a White Lady who rides near Hyghams. I had heard of this occurrence in the 1960s, when a local worthy told me that nothing would cross Hyghams after dark. A self-appointed ghost specialist assured me that Hyghams haunting lady was Dorcas Noble, who I refer to further in to the book under Littlewick Green. I suppose it's plausible enough, if indeed anything supernatural is plausible, and as ghosts are notoriously difficult to interview I shall leave the matter open to speculation.

Incidentally, I have heard that some people have had strange experiences in Dark Lane, Wargrave. After finding it my duty to enquire in all four pubs I could find no one with first-hand experience. I think probably the name has given rife to speculation.

There is also a Dark Lane down near Sidmouth. It is almost a tunnel, where the soft rock has been channelled by tide and weather, the trees on top almost touching each other. What a strange and uncanny place, and what a plethora of imaginative and baseless stories surrounding it.

5

Maidenhead

Shoppenhangers Manor Restaurant

One would have thought that a town like Maidenhead would have an overabundance of haunting tales, but not so.

I used to dine at Shoppenhangers occasionally, when I could afford it. I remember it gave me the impression of a baronial hall, but unfortunately the restaurant no longer exists in its original state. The building was once part of a thirteenth-century manor house and although little is left, much of the newer building is of architectural interest. In the early 1970s the figure of an old man in grey, silently gliding across the floor, shocked a waiter. The old man has been sighted several times since, but his appearances are very rare. As to who the old chap is, or was, there seems to be very little evidence. It is said that the figure walks at two o'clock in the morning, which is allegedly the time that a servant of the Tudor Lord fell to his death from a staircase. Obviously there is no record of this, it is pure conjecture.

The town also offers a strange little story regarding Maidenhead Thicket, involving a Chinese family that moved away from their comfortable Victorian abode because the dead returned at night. The house was at Hangman's Corner where a gibbet once stood. Horses often refused to pass the building.

Burchetts Green

Claude Duval's ghost is reputed to haunt a street, woodlands and a local house. This is unlikely but possible, as Maidenhead Thicket was a favourite venue of Duval. While Frenchman Claude, the ultra romantic highwayman is in no way as prolific as Dick Turpin, if a ghost attired in clothes similar to Claude's is sighted, the chances are a million to one that it is somebody else's spirit. I use a pub/restaurant in Camberley named after Claude Duval but I'm not sure if he ever visited the town.

Burchetts Green House is said to be haunted by Druids and there have been some strange cries coming from woods near Hall Place. Hall Place itself, a college for some time, claims a spooky coach and horses. And the *Old Berkshire Village Book*, by the Women's Institute, mentions the ghost of a servant who resides at Black Horse Lodge.

Burchetts Green, said to be haunted by Claude Duvall, a genuinely romantic highwayman.

There have been some supernatural experiences at the Bell in Maidenhead over the years.

Cockpole Green is haunted by a horse in chains.

Cockpole Green

Cockpole Green is midway between Henley and Reading and is supposedly haunted by a horse in chains. The spectral equine visitor is heard, but is never seen, on a track that leads to Putters Farm. I can trace no one who has experienced this phenomenon, but a chap in a pub claims that his father had heard it.

'It is the sound of a working horse,' he related. 'According to dad it puffs and blows and by the sound of the chains it is dragging something heavy,' he continued. What is strange is that the horse is reputed to be heard at midnight. Not a time when farm animals are usually employed.

There is also a rumour that the old farmhouse had a haunted room that was permanently locked.

Cookham

Cookham reputedly has a headless lady, but I could not trace her whereabouts. There is also a story of footsteps on a prefab roof. The steps and prefab have probably gone, as I first heard the story in the 1960s. Whiteladyes Lane is supposedly called after a ghostly nun that walks there. That's about it for Cookham; very disappointing for such an ancient village.

Holyport

Personally I was disappointed in graceful Holyport; I could discover nothing. This occasionally happens when one takes it for granted that ancient buildings are fertile ground for the supernatural.

A professional lady informed Jeff Nicholls that she was working in her office and got the distinct feeling of being watched. Looking up she saw a man in a black jacket. He had an official look about him and somehow gave off the impression that he was involved in some legal profession. The gentleman disappeared leaving his observer trying to rationalise things, possibly inhibited with a feeling of terror. The lady went on to explain that at this precise time she had an employee taking her to court for wrongful dismissal. She had little hope of winning the case and was very much in two minds whether or not to capitulate. For some reason she gained confidence, fought and won the case much against expectations. Also, she was sure that her ghostly legal visitor was in some way responsible for her success.

Angus Macnaughten tells of a house at Holyport, named Lynden Manor. One of Angus's cousins resided there with his mother. There was a door there that would never stay closed and a figure, gender unknown, was often seen in the same doorway. I am sorry there is nothing more to report here, which seems a pity. I've tried but failed to find Lynden Manor in 2010.

Hurley Ladye Place

A priory was built in this lovely village in 1086 by Geoffrey de Mandeville, who arrived with William the Conqueror. This bloody-minded, cruel and arrogant man was later rewarded by vast estates. He burned and pillaged his way across the country, promising troops for Stephen, then Matilda, and then Stephen again, and once again Matilda, exacting a higher price on every occasion. Finally a group of barons banded together to force him out. Shortly after the construction of Hurley Priory the Benedictine monks began enlarging the premises after much destruction (the Reformation). The magnificent Ladye Place was built in honour of the blessed Virgin Mary by Sir Richard Lovelace in 1558.

Sir Richard was made Baron Lovelace soon after, but the title ceased to exist in 1736.

A plot was hatched against the Catholic King, James II, in the crypt of Ladye Place by the supporters of William of Orange, the leader of the enterprise being Lord Lovelace. When William became king he was entertained by Lovelace in a magnificent style at Ladye Place. All was going well for Lovelace, but even with vast resources his extravagant, improvident lifestyle soon lead to debts. That caused the sale of some of the estate. The crypt was long thought to be the monk's burial place. An idea proven when the house was demolished in 1838 and the bodies of three Benedictine monks were discovered.

The house, later rebuilt in Edwardian style, was purchased with 20 acres of grounds by a Colonel Rivers-More in 1924. The Colonel was an archaeologist and was firmly in the belief that Editha, sister of Edward the Confessor was buried here. It was believed that the Grey Lady who had long haunted the premises was a spirit of Editha. The Colonel planned a series of excavations to unearth the coffin, but he was in fact to disturb the repose of various others.

The first appearance was a spectral monk clad in the brown Benedictine habit. The spirit indicated with gestures a fireplace in the house which he made signs to the Colonel to excavate. The digging mime was repeated in the indicated room by the monk the following day. It was soon discovered that the present fireplace was hiding a far larger and older one.

Excavations were redoubled in parts of the house. The original monk did not reappear. However, the party were joined by a second brother, named King. He also indicated the fireplace and by some form of mind reading he informed the Colonel that he had stolen a small box of gems and cast it down a well, hoping to retrieve it later. The Colonel spent some time clearing centuries of rubbish from the well and finally found the casket, complete with a small amount of jewels at the bottom. Brother King returned, appearing satisfied, and then disappeared forever.

Colonel Rivers-More now greatly convinced that he was near to Editha's grave, set about his excavations with renewed vigour. His quest lasted twenty-three years, involving family, friends and neighbours.

There was no shortage of spectral monk's. An early visitation appeared to the Colonel's brother-in-law and several more apparitions of monks appeared to various guests, friends and volunteers. One lady, badly affected by a visitation, tried to insist that the Colonel have the place exorcised. The Colonel paid no notice increasingly more and more monks turned up; one in particular was a smiling chap who kept his arms folded.

King James II.

Finally, the Colonel was convinced that calling in a medium might even help to find Editha's tomb and so a séance took place. The monks did their best to help; many were communicated with, including one that confessed to black magic. Another spectral monk was helpful indeed, describing where they should dig to find the priory's original footings. Working to the monk's directions they discovered a hard base surrounded by tiles. There was much excitement when it revealed a shrine containing human remains, but sadly though, not those of Editha.

Spiralling costs finally forced the Colonel to cease excavations and in 1947 Ladye Place was put up for auction. Editha's whereabouts were never discovered. The house was sold and divided into three. The monks ceased to materialise and Editha, if she ever was there, reposes with the brothers, hopefully in a chaste and undefiled condition.

Also in Hurley is the Olde Bell pub. When I first started frequenting pubs, at the age of thirteen (I was a big lad), one of the earliest I cycled to was the Olde Bell. The inn is one of a dozen claimants for the oldest in England. The building has parts that date back to 1133, but most of the present architecture is fifteenth or sixteenth century.

There is some evidence that there was once an even older building here, probably providing food and sustenance to the aforementioned monks and their guests. This would add weight to the notion of a suspected tunnel that is thought to exist between the two buildings. The tunnel that is rumoured to start by the fireplace has been closed for years, but it is from here that murmurings and chantings have occasionally been heard. One American, staying here in the mid-1970s, described the chantings as exceedingly peaceful, a sort of solace, support and consolation. There has been little heard recently.

Knowl Hill

The Bird in Hand, a most attractive hostelry on the A4 is reputedly haunted by a highwayman who met his demise by falling down the stairs in a drunken stupor. For some reason he is named Captain Jack, which is probably a far more recent nickname.

Not far down the A4, one comes across the equally attractive Seven Stars. The story here is similar to the Bird in Hand. The only difference is that the spiritual highwayman here mounted the stairs seated upon his steed; his intent was to steal the landlord's daughter. His mission was all but accomplished, when he was fatally shot in the back by one of the landlord's employees.

Littlewick Green

There are three ghosts that apparently inhabit Littlewick Green: Dorcas Noble, the White Lady and the white dog of Feens; their names are just about all that is known of them. I tried to dig a little deeper with little success. Of the White Lady I could find next to nothing, only that she haunts the woods on a white steed.

Dorcas Noble came from quite an affluent family. She dabbled in witchcraft and used the black art to find her ex-lover, who had forsaken her. Thinking he was hiding from her she called on the coven to magic her into his arms. Unfortunately for Dorcas, her lover was dead, but the spell still worked and she joined him. The ghost of Dorcas is seen on paths near the A4 riding a white horse, searching for her lover who was killed whilst hunting.

The White Dog of Feens often haunts in conjunction with Dorcas. Feens has been suggested as Dorcas's house. The White Dog's lonely and chilling call often announces his mistress's appearance. I wonder, could the White Lady be another duplicate of the same woman? Who knows?

The Seven Stars, Knowl Hill is home to a phantom highwayman.

Money Row Green

The White Hart at Money Row Green has two ghosts, an internal one and an external one. The internal ghost is another Grey Lady. Her appearances were quite prolific just after the Second World War, but like many others they have been rare of late. She seems to be quite a cheerful spook and she definitely has a preference for Christmas time. The Grey Lady differs from her many sisters in one respect; she has a baby in her arms. However, the lady's origin is unknown. In living memory no woman or child has died at the inn, so the lady and child will remain mysteries.

The external ghost that passes the White Hart is another equine one. Again more often heard than seen, it is reputed to be Kruger, who was killed while racing at nearby Hawthorn Hill in 1901. Why the spectre should choose to haunt this stretch of road is unknown.

Oakley Green

If you could see the Oakley Court Hotel you would be in no doubt as to why it was selected by Hammer House of Horrors to be seen at the start of all their releases. It is now a magnificent hotel belonging to a group that maintains the very highest standards. It was built in 1858 by the very eccentric Sir Robert Saye. The Gothic building is bizarre indeed; twisted towers and strange archways are guarded by ominous and weird gargoyles. Caught on a misty day it gives a feeling of vague terror, hence Hammer's choice. However, tales by local correspondents that its vista has encouraged people to commit suicide in the Thames are greatly exaggerated.

During the Second World War, the Government lent it to the French Resistance, during which time tales of the hauntings were most prolific. The supernatural happenings were varied and vivid, so much so that it was impossible to get in staff locally. The events were too numerous to reveal here.

From the mid-1950s to the mid-1970s, the building was left derelict. If scary when occupied, after twenty years of vacancy, which did nothing for its charm or reputation, it looked grotesque and moribund.

Remenham

Mary Blandy, a thirty-year-old spinster from Henley, was convicted of the murder of her father and hanged in 1752. Her accomplice and loyal fiancée, captain Willie Cranstoun, did a runner over to France.

Mary administered arsenic to her father, however, some doubt her guilt. But having read several books on the subject I personally am convinced that justice was done. Mary, a sort of local heroine in Henley, is said to haunt three sites. One is the family's house in Hart Street, another is the Kenton Theatre, where, when The Hanging Wood, a story concerning Mary, is being produced, poltergeist activity regularly occurs. Small things like curtains and lights play up. I've had little dealings with amateur theatrics but, in my limited experience, a host of inexplicable happenings occurring regularly is not unusual. As the first two haunted sites are over the Thames in Oxfordshire our interest lies with the third one in Remenham.

While waiting for the results of an autopsy, Mary was under a sort of house arrest, which meant she was confined to her bedroom. Having been incarcerated there for a couple of days, Mary was pleasantly surprised to find her door accidentally unlocked and decided

Oakley Court Hotel.

The Little Angel, Remenham is supposedly haunted by Mary Blandy, the Henley murderess.

upon a walk. As she teetered across the market (her shoelaces and buckles had been confiscated) she was quickly recognized.

'There goes Mary Blandy, the murderess,' screamed a tradeswoman, aiming some rotten fruit at her; obviously her guilt had already been decided.

'Catch the poisoner, she's escaping,' or words to that effect split the air. Mary ran in the direction of Henley Bridge, her flight greatly hampered by her long dress and loose shoes. The hue and cry was up, and bombarded by fruit and vegetables and chased by a shouting mob, progress across the bridge seemed endless. The mob was closing in and becoming wilder and more revengeful by the minute. Finally, on reaching the Berkshire side of the bridge a bloodstained and shoeless Mary entered the Little Angel. The inn was owned by a friend of hers and after hammering on the window until her small hands bled she was finally admitted and the door barred behind her. The howling mob outside was finally dispersed by Richard Fisher, the town Constable.

Mary Blandy was no longer permitted house arrest; that night she was taken by coach to prison in Oxford where she was heavily shackled until her trial, conviction and subsequent execution. Some time later there were reports of strange frantic tappings on the window of the Little Angel. On inspection no one was there. They continued periodically for centuries, and some say they still do.

6

Slough

SLOUGH in general is somewhat short of ghosts, perhaps because little of the town is old and rich with history. The town is, however, surrounded by charismatic villages, but even these have little to report where the supernatural is concerned. Such villages as Chalvey and Chippenham have been swallowed up and have totally lost their individuality. Ditton Park, actually in Langley, another swallowed village, has several reports of spooks.

A well-known story concerns a gardener called Meades. Meades was working while some large rebuilding contract was taking place. The gardener's story would seem to be an example of a time slip, for he described how he witnessed a mediaeval funeral. I have heard that the era was verified by the gardener being taken to a local museum where he picked out pictures showing people in similar clothing.

Back to Mr Meades story. He described a procession of monks carrying a coffin adorned by a sword and shield. There were also soldiers dressed in a sort of uniform including armour and boots, following the mourning monks. The cortège stopped quite abruptly and then vanished. Meades had the presence of mind, not to mention the courage,

to pinpoint where the coffin finally rested. His story must have been believed, because he convinced the authorities to excavate the site. It was not long before they discovered the remains of an ancient chapel. I have not been able to verify this strange little story, but I believe there is quite a worthwhile amount of truth here. It is far too fanciful to believe that the large programme of alterations taking place forced the cortege to relocate the coffin from its original resting place, perhaps to find a safer place for internment, but who knows.

While in the vicinity, Langley Church and the nearby almshouse are worth a brief look. According to Mr Macnaughten, the almshouses were used by evacuees during the Second World War. This caused a local old lady to take umbrage. She took the position that almshouses were intended for the elderly and should remain so, whatever outside circumstances were being experienced. The old lady swore to plague the inhabitants in life and haunt them when deceased and this she did.

True to her word, the old girl made regular appearances. One particular terrified couple incurred her wraith on a regular basis and awoke one night with a feeling of sudden coldness. They discovered that their mattress had been turned from the bed and the old lady stood there smirking. It seems that their unwanted spectral guest had summoned a great deal of strength since her demise. She was also blamed for sliding a heavy wardrobe across the floor. Finally, there was some sort of exorcism, which seemed to drain the old girl's ardour for revenge. Nothing else was seen of her.

Elsewhere in Slough, Upton Court was a very old house indeed and of recent times had been associated with small firms and local newspapers. When I enquired as to a strange apparition some ten years ago, I was told that the lady with the bloodstained nightdress still made fairly regular appearances. Upton Court was rented in Victorian times by the famous journalist Augustus Sala. At that time the blood-soaked lady had been around for at least 300 years. Sala took a rather flippant attitude to his spectral lady, but his staff members were far more concerned; he found it difficult to keep any longer than a month. On a visit to Upton Court in 2010 I found it to be now derelict.

Cippenham Place, a large old building, has yet another procession of cowled monks carrying a coffin. The ghostly cortege only appears on one particular day of the year. It is sometime in May and falls on the date of the death of a previous owner, who drowned to death. For some unknown reason the spectral coffin circumnavigates the house three times.

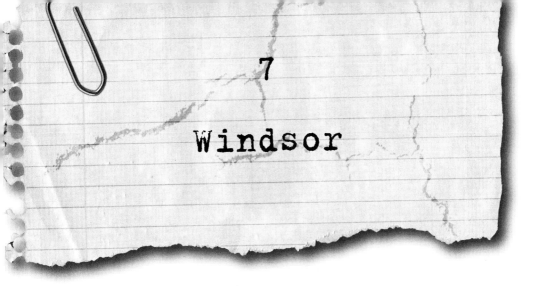

Windsor

AS I mentioned in my introduction, it is not my intention to rehash well-known ghost stories; it has been done far too often. However, it would be impossible not to mention the well-established ones. Windsor Castle reputedly has ten or a dozen resident ghosts. Let us begin with the royal personages.

Queen Elizabeth I. There have been several sightings of good Queen Bess. Described as a tall striking woman, her most celebrated appearance was to an army officer, Lieutenant Carr Glynn, in 1897. Glynn witnessed the apparition in the castle's library where she strode the length of the building before entering an inner room and disappearing before the eyes of the startled Lieutenant. Several of Queen Victoria's children reported sightings; ghost hunts were one of their favourite games. Another report came from the Empress Frederica Germaine who not only described an appearance, but also heard the tapping of the Queen's high heels.

Apparently Good Queen Bess is not alone in the Royal library; the honoured chamber is also frequented by King George III. Visitors to the Royal library suddenly hear the words 'What! What?' whispered in their ears. These words were basically the only phrases uttered by mad King George III. Poor mad George was confined to Windsor Castle and not treated particularly well. The library was one of the few rooms left at his disposal, but even here he was continually under observation. However, he did once escape to chase Fanny Burney around a tree in the Green Park. Perhaps George's spirit finds solace in the undisturbed library.

Our third Royal ghost is the colourful and charismatic Henry VIII. On several occasions in living memory Henry has been witnessed walking the battlements. He is described as strolling with his hands behind his back and then suddenly, he turns and disappears through a wall. Speculators have taken the trouble to trace old plans of the castle and there seems to be no doubt that there was once a door where Henry vanishes.

Robust Henry is also thought to haunt the cloisters. This time he is heard rather than seen. There is a low groan and the sound of Henry dragging his gout ravaged foot.

And now Charles I, our final royal ghost. Charles I was another spectre fascinated by the library, this time seen stroking his beard in a pensive mood and leaning on the back of a chair. Charles has also been witnessed in the Canons House, once again recognized by his distinctive beard.

Windsor Castle.

Henry VIII.

Henry VIII's daughter, Elizabeth I, one of the ghosts at Windsor Castle.

George Villiers, the first Duke of Buckingham, is reputed to haunt an area of Windsor Castle. Villiers was an evil and conniving man who sycophantically endeared himself to royalty. James I and his son Charles were espied and courted by Villiers. Villiers was murdered on 23 August 1628 at a Portsmouth inn by a trooper named John Felton. Felton became a public hero overnight, highly appreciated by a country that realised it had a lot to thank him for. Why Villiers spectre should return to Windsor Castle I do not know. Perhaps it is more comfortable than a modest inn on Portsmouth's Old High Street.

The ghost of William Wykeham is another visitor to Windsor Castle. Witnesses to the spirit of William Wykeham describe experiencing a sense of peace, tranquillity and a type of honest self-satisfaction.

Born at Wickham in Hampshire in 1324, Wykeham became surveyor of royal castles to Edward III. Obviously Wykeham spent much his time at Windsor where he was the architect of much of the fourteenth-century construction. His shade has been reported at night at the Round Tower, smiling innocuously and admiring the view.

Far less peaceful than Wykeham's Round Tower is the Curfew Tower. Built in 1319, it came to be used for executions. Prisoners were brought from the cells below and escorted to a door high up in the 100ft tall tower. There they were hanged from an outside beam, thereby giving a perfect warning view to the public. The stairs had a trip step, slightly wider than the rest. In the unlikely event of a felon breaking away from his escorts a trip step would cause him to stumble and impede his escape.

Incidentally, in his book *Our Mysterious Shire*, Jeff Nicholls informs us that the last man to be hanged from the beam here was a butcher from the town, named Mark Fytton.

The sounds of slow footsteps descending the stairs have been heard on many occasions.

There were several reports in the 1960s about some supernatural happenings around St George's Chapel. The chapel has a mysterious look about it that is often enhanced by moonlit cloudy skies. There was, however, one report from many years earlier that went into more detail.

A lady who lived at the Seabrook Tower at Windsor Castle in 1873 was walking home past St George's Chapel when she noticed statue like figures outside. She described it as a four figure group; three were kneeling and the fourth was standing and holding a sword, looking as though he was about to deliver the death blow to the kneeling three. On her return, the figures were no more; the lady made enquiries but to no avail. What can one say? We are far too late to interview the lady and who knows what games the mind can play?

Windsor's spectral Guardsman, possibly policeman, depending on the reports, is a stark enigma. If anything there is too much information. Let me try and put the sightings into some sort of chronological order; they are, to say the least, confusing.

A Guardsman is reported to have committed suicide by shooting himself in the Long Walk in 1927. Reputedly he had seen the area's most prolific ghost, Herne the Hunter. Weeks later another patrolling Guardsman noticed and recognized the spectre of his suicidal acquaintance. Reluctant to speak of his experience, the Guardsman kept it to himself until he learned that his colleague, who had performed the previous patrol, had also witnessed the shade of the dearly departed comrade.

Now complications set in, because twenty-one years previously, in 1906, a policeman had witnessed a spectral grenadier, as indeed had a Guardsman. There were also reports of two spectral guardsmen in uniform, or possibly policemen, standing side by side. The latest report, as recent as the 1970s, tells yet again of a serving soldier seeing a spooky guardsman at the same place exactly as where the guardsman committed suicide after encountering the ghost of Herne the Hunter. I trust all is clear now.

Other than Dick Turpin, Herne the Hunter of Windsor Great Park must be the most overworked and over reported spook in the country. Unlike Turpin, Herne is very much more geographically intense, keeping strictly to the above-mentioned Great Park and local forestry. Among hundreds of slightly varying reports I have seen a seventy page booklet on Herne alone. I shall attempt to be more brief.

Herne the Hunter has been around for some 500 years. In the Bard's *Merry Wives of Windsor* he is mentioned when Mrs Ford entices Falstaff to dress up as him. Harrison Ainsworth, a novelist responsible for portraying many villains as heroes, took Herne a little more seriously, describing him as a frightening and awesome figure.

In brief, Herne was a very favoured huntsman of Richard II. His knowledge of the forest and his tracking skills were second to none. One day the King, along with his hunting party, injured a large stag. The badly maimed animal made a last charge at the King. It would have, in all probability, been the death of the sovereign if a very quick thinking Herne had not leapt upon its back and cut its throat. The King was saved and Herne, though fatally wounded, became a hero.

Suddenly a tall stranger appeared and informed the King that he could save Herne's life. He was apparently once commanded to do so. The stranger stepped forward and cut the stag's antlers from its head before binding them to Herne's head. On his instruction a makeshift stretcher was constructed on which

the famous hunter was to be conveyed to the stranger's hut on Bagshot Heath. As he left, the King informed Herne that should he recover he would be made chief huntsman for the rest of his life.

On arrival at the stranger's hut the stretcher-bearers had been a little concerned about Herne's potential promotion. Consequently they found it prudent to take the stranger aside and make him an offer he couldn't refuse. In short, if Herne didn't die the stranger would. The stranger pointed out that he could not break his word to the King, but he could promise that all Herne's accumulated hunting skills and local knowledge would go. However, if he took this action Herne's curse would be with them forever.

Unafraid of such tittle-tattle, the huntsman ordered the stranger to proceed. Physically Herne recovered, and once again accompanied Richard II on the hunts, but he had lost his sense of hearing and smell. He could no longer find the animal lairs nor track the deer. The King, being appreciative of all Herne had done in the past sacked him and kicked him out to his house. A short time later, one of the conspirators discovered Herne's body hanging from a tree. He rushed to fetch the other hunters but when they returned the corpse had gone.

Shortly afterwards, the conspirators began to have tragic accidents. The King lost patience with them and cast several out of their homes. There was but one thing to do: a group of them set out to consult the Wizard of Bagshot Heath. They were informed that Herne's spirit inhabited the vast oak on which he hanged himself. They would have no peace until they had appeased Herne's unquiet spirit. The conspirators gathered under the vast oak at midnight and the first thing to appear was a purple vapour that manifested itself into the Wizard. It makes me wonder why a magician who could turn from vapour to skin and bones at will was afraid of being killed in the first place.

Next to appear was Herne astride a massive black horse. The stag's horns were now growing from the Hunter's head. He was a terrifying sight. He rode off ordering the frightened hunters to follow. They hunted all night completely obliterating every one of the forests deer. This of course did not please Richard II, who had all the hunters brought before him. Unbeknown to them, he had visited the mighty oak the night before and had spoken to Herne. The phantom hunter had assured him that if he punished the wrongdoers the deer would return and he would disappear during the King's lifetime. What could a reasonable King do?

Obviously he immediately executed all the offenders. The phantom hunter kept his promise and as if by magic, the day after the executions, deer began to frequent the forest and within a few weeks the Great Park had the most plentiful supply in the country.

Also, the day after Richard II's death the frightening spectre rode once more in the forest. The Herne's Oak has long since gone, but is still celebrated on a local pub sign. Herne himself still rides, and is scarier than ever before; he still has his horns but recent sightings say that his hair is now turned to flame and his enormous spectral horse is accompanied by a pack of hounds.

The sound of Herne's terrifying hunt was allegedly heard quite recently by two Eton schoolboys. Adding weight to this report, it is said that their experience took place exactly where Herne Oak originally stood, before it burnt down in 1863. The site is on a footpath leading from the Windsor Road to Queen Adelaide's Lodge.

M—— Cottage is an ancient house near the centre of Windsor town. I had heard of it in my youth but had never found an excuse to gain entry. Joan Forman in her *The Haunted South* seemed to have success and tells us of the feeling of animosity and hostility that seemed to prevail from a certain room. The owner described to Joan how a guest saw a tall man with a dark cloak on several occasions. The guest finally enquired who the man was, but nobody knew. The tall man seems to have been the only sighted ghost in situ, but various members of the family had heard the names called out from time to time.

There would also seem to be a form of time slip here. Members of the family heard or experienced the feeling of an unseen battle here; it was a clamour or some sort of commotion. The site is thought to have once been the scene of the confrontation between Romans and Britons. If M—— Cottage still exists, it is obviously a private dwelling, so one must respect privacy here.

Thames Street in Windsor is full of old houses, one of which had an evil reputation. It is said to have once been the dwelling place of Cardinal Wolsey after he fled Windsor Castle in disgrace after incurring the wraith of Henry VIII. Perhaps it was Wolsey's intention to keep a low profile until Henry cooled down. Henry didn't and Wolsey died in disgrace before he could be tried for treason.

The old house was once reputed to be an inn and also a shop. Shop assistants were reputedly often nudged and tapped on the

Herne the Hunter.

shoulder, but this is hearsay from literally centuries ago. More recently, workers at the castle were lodged here, but apparently they were far from pleased with the accommodation. A feeling of deep depression was rife and several tenants felt a strong urge to throw themselves down the stairwell. Others shared nightmares of a horrible old man dragging his leg behind him (surely this can't be Henry with his gout again?).

Just to finish, there were murmurings from the cellar which is thought was once part of the chapel. The floor was lifted and the charred remains of several babies were discovered; they were again interred with a Christian service.

I have mentioned Sir Christopher Wrens House Hotel in book form before, but as it is my intention to mention every spook I've ever heard of in Old Berkshire, I couldn't leave her out. Despite its name there is precious little evidence that Christopher Wren ever set foot in the building. The romantic style and undeniable ambience here belies a rather chequered history.

Once a private dwelling, the house was owned by a family named Cheshire. Allegedly this unlucky family was struck down by a mysterious illness, which was prevalent in foreign parts; but these were countries that the family had never visited. Also one of the daughters became pregnant, a truly unpardonable sin in the 1800s. It is thought that the young lady had a mental breakdown. It is open to conjecture whether this was a reasonable excuse to confine her to her room. But her only respite was to be let out into the walled garden very late at night or early in the morning.

Whether it was by accident or intent Mr Cheshire nearly died from food poisoning shortly after his daughter's confinement. Incidentally, the illegitimate child died in early infancy. Bad luck seemed to stick to Mr

Cheshire; his finances rapidly decreased and the family moved to a small property. His other daughter, engaged to a peer, was jilted at the last moment. Perhaps her intended was put off by the failing finances and the suspect mental stability of the family.

The scourge, however, seemed attached to the house rather than the family and over the next 100 years, families came and went in quick succession – the place had earned a reputation of being haunted. One shade was the unfortunate daughter wandering in the garden, and there was also something uncanny and inexplicable in the house.

In the 1900s, the house was purchased by Baroness Vaux who used it as a summer residence. However, she could not keep any staff; all left after a few days, stating that parts of the house had an unbearable atmosphere. After the Baroness's departure the old place stayed empty for many years. In 1930 the house was bought by two sisters with the unusual surname of Outlaw. While admitting that the house was probably haunted, the sisters stayed put, firstly opening the premises as a teashop and then as a hotel.

In another story Mr Macnaughten tells of a levelheaded ex-CID officer who lived in a flat in an eighteenth-century house in Sheet Street. He had retired for the night when he heard heavy breathing. Sitting up in bed he noticed a figure of a short man, who could have been naked. Only the torso, head and arms could be seen. The body had a type of sheen to it and for some reason the observer suspected that his visitor may be a victim of leprosy. We are not informed as to how long the spectral visitor remained, but it disappeared with the turning on of the bedside lamp, leaving the observer with his hair literally standing on end.

Angus Macnaughten also has an expert knowledge of Hadleigh House because he once lived there. His mother experienced several strange happenings, not the least of which was a bolt on the inside of the door that embedded itself in. There was also a prevailing scent of clove carnations, an aroma that could be distinguished on regular occasions, even though such flowers were never in the house. There were also numerous strange knockings and tappings coming from various rooms.

The same gentleman witnessed a strange procession in the garden of Abbey House (now demolished). He described the figures as being indistinct, but remembered one figure in particular. It was a man with a tall hat and a large white collar. The entourage disappeared as quickly as it had materialised, possibly a cortège – we shall never know.

Clewer

An ancient village indeed, but for a long time now it has been swallowed up by its larger neighbour, Windsor. Many servants of the Royal Castle have been borne down the hill to Clewer churchyard. Here under a white cross lies the body of Sir Thomas Biddulph, Queen Victoria's keeper of the Prince's purse. Amongst other inhabitants is good old Arabella Bridgeman, who passed away at the age of 107. The Clewer churchyard is inundated with the briefly famous, but I can find no reports of the supernatural. In a location that lends itself to be alive with ghosts (if one pardons a contradiction in terms), this is most strange.

Nick Brazil in his *A Journey with Ghosts* interviewed a friend of his who in the past attended the nurses training college at Clewer. The college had a resident ghost named Emily, who was accepted and seemed to be a benign and friendly spirit. Nick's friend relates that one night, a colleague at the college named Erica was suffering from a raucous cough. As their rooms were in close proximity to each other the cough was affecting the first lady's studies. One night she was pleased to hear approaching footsteps and a knock on Erica's door. Slowly the coughing ceased and the teller of the story assumed that her friend had received a glass of water. When in the morning she congratulated Erica on finally receiving something for her cough she denied all knowledge of the visit and the water. Approaching the night staff with the same enquiry she found that they endorsed Erica's denial. It must have been Emily.

Further exploits of Emily were to regularly open and close windows and doors, totally against the authority's orders. There is also a rather distressing episode when Emily seems to have tried to get into bed with one of the nurses. Who this rather active ghost was before she crossed the void is unknown. Perhaps, however, Emily is just a helpful nurse, as such familiarities are not unusual when referring to a friendly spirit.

The Church of England's Children's Society Home once thrived at Clewer. It was run by the sisterhood of St John the Baptist. Sadly the old building has since been demolished. In living memory, however, a tale exists that one room had such a malevolent and malicious atmosphere that it was untenable. Nobody would sleep there and the cleaners would only enter in pairs. The atmosphere is blamed on a nun who hanged herself in the surrounding park. Why her shade should move into the house one can but wonder.

Colnbrook

The story of the Ostrich (once the Hospice) has been more often related than any other. It is one of those unfortunate tales that is copied from one account to the other with such rapidity that no one bothers to check the few facts that are known. With this story I will be brief.

The Ostrich first came to light with the nefarious affairs of the landlord Jarman, probably in the late fifteenth century. It is mentioned in a Thomas Deloney novel in the late 1500s. The landlord devised a bed that he could upend with a gadget below, thereby tipping the unfortunate occupant through the floor and into a barrel of boiling fat. It must have been a horrible death – but a profitable one for the landlord, who apparently helped himself to any riches the visitor had left in their clothes when retiring for the night.

Deloney had Jarman's transgressions discovered and the hospice raised to the ground. He also had the landlord and his wife executed at Reading for over thirty murders. What on earth did they do with the bodies? Why was no one ever missed? Answer, most of the murders were fictitious. There was one gentleman whose body was traced, a man

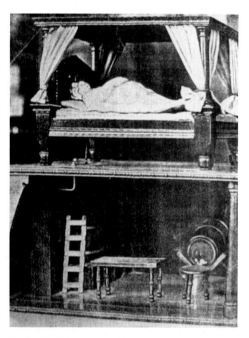

The Ostrich, Colnbrook. A working model details the system used in many murders.

named Cole. It is also rumoured that the poor man was found in a brook, hence Colnbrook, but this is most unlikely. There were, however, several disappearances in the region of the Hospice (Ostrich) and there is some evidence that the landlord was apprehended when a traveller got up to answer a call of nature and noticed his bed going up at a 45° angle. The visitor, probably in a state of undress, clambered out of the window and flagged down a coach.

Another story tells how a stable lad heard screaming from the cellar and discovered Jarman trying to wipe spattered fat from his face with victim feet-up in the barrel nearby.

I've no doubt whatsoever that the landlord murdered several people here, but there is no record of the hangings. I first called at the Ostrich in 1960; the landlord showed me a working model of the death contraption; it was well made and I was impressed. He was full of the story, most of it impossible.

Firstly Deloney used the story in a novel, which by his own admission was grossly exaggerated – nobody knew the notorious landlords name. Jarman was an invention of Deloney's.

I was amused recently when I saw on a TV programme a well-known ghost-hunter/ medium talking to a ghost named Jarman. I was pleased to see that the Ostrich's landlord had adopted his fictitious name many years after his demise. What a load of old waffle – mediums will be talking to Pickwick, Long John Silver or Alice in Wonderland soon.

Just to add to this misconception, the ghost of the Ostrich is reputed to be Cole, one of the unfortunate victims. Just a note before leaving the Ostrich: I was being interviewed by a local BBC radio station some six or seven years ago; the programme was nearly over when the interviewer finalised by asking me if I knew how the landlord was caught. I thought I'd be comical before such a vast audience and so I chirped up with, 'Well you see, they got him for no VAT returns.'

'Surely not,' he replied, 'VAT didn't come in until late in the twentieth century.'

Oh well, that joke fell on stony ground.

Datchet

Datchet is a beautiful little riverside village, a favourite with Shakespeare and a small gem in sight from Windsor Castle. The Bard made Datchet Mead, the scene of Sir John Falstaff's ducking. The Royal Stag is an attractive old pub well in-keeping with its surroundings. It stands opposite Datchet's picturesque church that has a bearing on our story.

The Royal Stag has a strange and unusual story indeed; strange yes, but quite well attested also. It was a cold and snow-filled day in a harsh winter towards the end of Queen Victoria's long reign. A local labourer who was said to be making his way to Taplow had taken his young son to work with him. On his return he called into the Royal Stag while his son played cheerfully amid the snow in the churchyard. After some time of enjoying the snow, the boy was getting wet and cold. Walking the few yards to the inn, he tapped on the window to attract his father's attention, but unfortunately for the boy his father was well in his cups and having a good time with his friends; he was oblivious to anything else. Shortly afterwards the boy, now suffering from cold and exposure, leant upon the window and then sank down the wall to his death in the snow, leaving a pathetic, yet indelible handprint on the window pane.

Over the years, the handprint has reappeared on a fairly regular basis. Sometimes the print lasts for weeks and at others for a mere few minutes. In 1979 a national newspaper removed the pane, complete with handprint and took it away for examination.

Various experiments were carried out on the object, but after a long analysis little or nothing was learned. What did seem strange however was that the handprint appeared on a new pane that had been substituted in the original frame. It is also alleged that when a photograph of the handprint, taken by a local author, was placed on the bar, glasses and bottles fell from shelves onto the floor. Naturally, the landlord forbade such an action to be repeated.

It is strange for me to try and imagine such a happening – a boy, reputedly of five or six years old, being too shy to knock on the inn door when suffering from extreme cold. Admittedly, in Victorian days children were far more afraid of upsetting their parents' awesome tempers. Had I left my son outside while I indulged myself, he would have been kicking the door every three minutes and demanding refills of coke and crisps.

Apart from the inexplicable handprint, there are more inexplicable events associated with the Royal Stag. Footsteps and mumbling sounds have been heard in the cellar, which incidentally contains the tombstone of William Herbert. Apparently, if the stone is removed it returns of its own volition. How it got there in the first place is unknown. There is also a haunted bedroom, occasionally occupied by a tall man with grey hair and a large hooked nose. Finally, there are reports from a babysitter of a toilet that flushed itself on several occasions.

Eton College

This home of academia is also the home of more supernatural visitations per square mile than anywhere else in the country.

Mr H.E. Luxmoore was a famous master here for many years. After his demise his colleagues and friends erected a pavilion

Eton College.

Eton schoolboys regularly searched for the college's numerous ghosts.

dedicated to him in what had become known as Luxmoore's Garden, a strip of ground in which he had created flowerbeds and other features. Obviously, the dignified celebration was recorded by a local photographer. When the photos were developed, Luxmoore, complete with stick, cape and flowing white hair, could clearly be seen. The photograph kept in a shop in Eton High Street was verified and endorsed by several of his closest friends who had attended the occasion.

The above story is quite well known and attested to at the college. Angus Macnaughten tells us of another photograph of the chapel taken in the 1950s. An old couple, complete with walking sticks, may be discerned, although the photographer swears that there was nobody about at the time.

Other less well-known sightings at the college include the Vice Provosts Lodge where ghostly footsteps mount the stairs. Allegedly, a lady living there often called out to the phantom to enter, but he or she never accepted the invitation.

I was told of a college-owned house on the Slough Road that once had some mild inexplicable experiences. I made some brief enquiries but was told the house no longer existed. An Eton boy's boarding house in Keates Lane has also been demolished. There was some slight poltergeist activity there in the 1920s. There was also an exorcism, the result of which is unknown.

A cloaked figure is apparently still around the college grounds. It frequents various courts and buildings in the complex but has been seen more often crossing the playing fields. Many investigators find the report more than a little suspect; boys will be boys.

Probably Eton College's most famous spectre is Jane Shore. Jane was the lover of Edward IV and was beloved by Eton because she persuaded the King from demolishing it. Edward IV hated the place merely because it was founded by Lancastrian Henry VI. The college was forever grateful and when Jane fell from favour with Edward and was left penniless and imprisoned, Eton came to her aid. The Provost and fellows secured her release from prison and supplied her with a room in Lupton's Tower. Jane died there in 1526.

Jane Shore haunts various parts of Eton including the cloisters and her home, Lupton's Tower. Although she is a friendly spirit she terrified one College journalist by following him too closely one evening. He was reputed to have been approached by a lady in a dark mediaeval dress. It was a few minutes before he realised that there was something mystical about the figure. As it neared with a floating action the gentleman felt it time to leave. It is possible that Jane and the figure in the cloak are one and the same. Who knows?

Eton High Street

The Old Cockpit on the Eton High Street has been around since the fifteenth century and it is ironic that such a picturesque old building was the scene of literally thousands of barbaric cockfights. The original cockpit, with its remains behind the building, is one of the few to survive in the country. Even now it is easy to imagine the screaming shouting sportsmen as they bet on which bird would tear the other one to bits.

With all the colourful goings on, it is strange to relate that the spirit here is a gentle, mild and nearly apologetic little lady in grey attire that politely passes between the tables. It is possible that the lady's friendly manner has prevented any attempts at exorcism over the years.

Nearby, the spirit of a woman in a shop flat has been witnessed walking 18in above the floor. On investigation it was discovered that the floor was once much higher.

The Watermans Arms, Eton, built
on the tomb of plague victims.

Another shop is, or was, haunted by a young man who committed suicide by cutting his throat with a razor.

A local antique shop was haunted by the ghost of the owner, who was killed by a car. He had left his worldly goods to his staff and they helped themselves as instructed. It would appear that the owner remained as his footsteps were often heard. The family that moved in found the building had an ominous, creepy feeling about it. The family decided to burn and destroy all that was left of the original owner's belongings. Some reports state that he did not go quietly – something unseen but not unheard threw a tantrum, throwing itself about the bedroom and tearing the bedclothes.

Finally, as far as we know, we have a friendly little man known as 'The Doctor'. When I first heard of this pleasant little spook in the 1960s, The Doctor was part of living memory.

Clad in a brown coat and trilby he went from door to door visiting patients.

The Waterman's Arms is my favourite watering hole in Eton. Like many pubs, the owners decided that the means of survival was to invest in a restaurant, a very large restaurant. I was pleased to see that most of the old paintings, prints and photographs still remain in *situ*. However, what seemed to be strange was a map or chart of the river on the ceiling adorned by various postcards of riverside scenes in the appropriate places. The whole ambience of the Waterman's Arms is a pleasant one. What was it then that made grumbling and moaning noises that seemed to come from the very depth of the Earth in such an attractive venue? When the inn was built in 1542, its original purpose was a plague house. The dead, and some that were not quite dead, were brought down the river on rafts to be interred. Please relax with your pint; nothing has been heard for a couple of decades.

Old Windsor

One spirit here concerns a house at Priest Hill in which the occupier, seventy-five years ago, committed suicide by tying a lawn-mower around his neck and jumping into the Thames. However, he seems not to haunt his earthly premises. A Ouija board experiment named a girl called Sally. Angus Macnaughten informs us of the house where footprints were burnt into the lino.

The Fox and Castle was a Christmas card inn, with its white walls and twisted exposed timbers. Sadly it was closed when I went to visit it some years ago. The name was unique, but in a book I wrote in the '90s I had a stab at it. The 'castle' part is obvious as its situation is close to the royal residence. The 'fox' part I believe has nothing to do with your four legged, handsome nomad, instead it refers to Charles James Fox, an eighteenth-century colourful politician who saw no harm in climbing his way up the social ladder by rubbing shoulders with royalty. His PR man got him introduced at the castle. It is said that he once sat in a Soho inn with his wig pulled over his eyes, pretending to be a Tory.

Fox was a survivor, a man for all seasons. He so much impressed Sam House, the Soho landlord that he gave free beer to all his customers who promised to vote for his gregarious, hedonistic but insincere hero. It is thought that after a long and vibrant political career Fox retired and purchased Sam House's Soho pub. Hopefully, the world famous Intrepid Fox pub still remains in London's Wardour Street.

The strange stories of the Fox and Castle were related to me by the landlord some twenty years ago. The stories are varied indeed. We have petrified dogs, phantom footmen and servants and a weeping small girl, who may or may not be the owner of an old shoe found in a forgotten fireplace.

Have these colourful appearances disappeared due to the destruction or vast alterations at the building? Sadly, probably so.

While in Old Windsor the modified, riverside Bells of Ousley is worth a visit. The ghosts here are not exactly in the building; it is a group of monks who float bells on a raft down the River Thames. The story goes that during Henry VIII's Reformation some bells at nearby Ousley were held at the monastery there. As the building was under threat of destruction the brothers decided to transport the bells to a small island on the Thames near Old Windsor. Under cover of darkness, the monks moved the bells to the raft and set off from the bank. History suggests that the raft capsized, spilling the monks and cargo to the bottom of the river. No one survived and the bells were never retrieved, at which I am surprised, as the river is neither wide nor deep at this point.

Also, I have tried to trace Ousley but there seems to be no record of it in the near vicinity. However, I have come across the vestiges of a village known locally as Ousley just above Henley in the foothills of the Chilterns.

8

Bracknell

EMBLEMS was once believed to be the most haunted house in Bracknell, but unfortunately it no longer exists. Situated by the Bagshot Road, it was an attractive nineteenth-century abode. The house was part and parcel of a nursery run by Walter Callingham, a much respected and capable gardener. Callingham had close associations with Wellington College at Crowthorne and presented the College with a giant redwood that can still be seen today. A sister tree, another giant redwood, was planted at Emblems. Callingham was succeeded at Emblems by a philatelist – little is known of the man except that he was small, frail and suffered permanent ill-health. In 1942 this gentleman's ill health deteriorated and he met his demise in that year.

There were various owners of the vast old house until 1957 when it was bought by Bracknell Development Corporation and rented to the *Bracknell News*. In 1960 I was a freelance cub reporter for the *Bracknell News* and spent quite a lot of time at Emblems. Naturally I was inflicted by its ghost stories. A young secretary that worked there was often surprised to hear footsteps on the stairs above her, although she knew very well that there was no one else in the building. When

she reported this to old members of staff and world weary journalists such as myself we all adopted the laid-back approach and said, 'It's only Clarence, he's harmless.' Clarence's footsteps were a very regular occurrence over nearly a decade. It would seem that Clarence was not only attracted by the aura and ambience created by adventurous, fearless and egotistical journalists, he was also heard by a site surveyor who was using Emblems as an office before its final obliteration.

Arriving very early one morning, the surveyor heard footsteps several flights above his adapted office. Thinking it to be burglars he armed himself with a shovel and proceeded upstairs. He searched the place thoroughly but found nothing. He then returned to his desk to continue some paperwork; he reported that the footsteps continued for nearly a minute.

Two years later a local author and supernatural investigator, complete with two friends, spent the night at Emblems. They experienced a drop in temperature in parts of the upper storeys. Also, in the morning, a tape recorder revealed a sharp bang followed by slow shuffling footsteps. Is it too fanciful to believe these were the phantom footsteps of the doddering, infirm philatelist finding it hard to sever all communications with his much loved home?

Old Farm, another house in Bracknell, had two if not three in-house ghosts. Over many years, a young girl (seven or eight years old) had been witnessed in the house and garden. She would seem to be a sociable young lady and might have gone unnoticed among her living counterparts had she not always been attired in a summer dress. The young supernatural visitor was also witnessed in the company of another young girl of a similar age. More rarely, the girls were seen playing while being scrutinised by an ancient lady, thought to be their grandmother.

It is time now for a tour of Bracknell's haunted licensed premises, beginning with the Hinds Head. Unfortunately this romantic and ghostly Bracknell pub no longer exists. But at one point it had a notorious landlord named Milliard. The story goes that he and his wife would ply travellers with drink before putting them to bed. When the couple considered their lodger comatose by ale they would pull a lever that would tip the bed to 45°, sliding its slumbering occupant into a well.

I hate to be a killjoy, but a much better authenticated account of such action names the Ostrich at Colnbrook as the venue of similar atrocities. Reports of the Milliard's activities are said to have taken place in the eighteenth century, but no specific dates are given – this is very vague. Try as I may I can find no record of the Milliards being hanged in Berkshire. If they were it must have been very early in the eighteenth century where records are a little scant. I have read a report of a Bracknell Yearbook from 1832 where it is stated that bones were discovered in a well. There is, however, no evidence that would qualify these as human bones. It was more than likely that the well, which was outside the building, was the last resting place of many of the town's unwanted pets. The well water probably put body remnants in the landlord's cellars and complemented his ale.

I was never quite able to discover who or what haunted the Hinds Head but something definitely did. There is no doubt that there was an underground passage of large dimensions there. It was discovered at the time of the demolition when an underpass beneath a roundabout was in the process of construction. It definitely led under the road to the Old Manor and possibly to the Bull further down the High Street. The Old Manor still stands, and thrives, now being part of a massive chain of licensed premises.

There is more than a vestige of the original ancient ambience here, an indestructible atmosphere. The Old Manor was privately owned by an Ascot veterinary surgeon until 1930. It was then purchased by a brewer and obtained a licence. The brewer apparently inherited the long in *situ* ghost.

During the religious persecutions, the Old Manor's several priest holes were in regular use. A very un-substantiated story tells us that a priest was discovered and slain here. Supposedly a cassock adorned figure that gazes down on drinkers from a lofty hole in the wall is an effigy of the poor fellow. He is definitely held responsible for the low murmurings that have been interpreted as a priest in prayer over many years. Stuck behind his barred grill watching others imbibe for decades, would be enough to cause this moaning and bleating. No doubt watching the Old Manor's second ghost must exasperate his situation. Bert, a regular for many years, still drops in the odd pint thirty years after his demise.

The Horse and Groom on the Bagshot Road near the centre of Bracknell has been a national steak house for a number of years now. To compliment the owners, they have kept most of its original old-world charm.

The Old Manor, Bracknell is haunted by several spirits.

South Hill Park's veranda, where the shade of Major Rickman walks.

I came across an interesting little story here while studying papers from 1810 in Reading Library. In that year an inquest was held at the inn concerning a young man who was murdered in the vicinity. William Ware, a lad of seventeen, was returning to his home at Frimley after visiting Bracknell Fair, accompanied by his father and two of his friends. Crossing Bagshot Heath, the party was set upon by three men with cudgels, thought to be Irishmen. The party was so severely beaten that they made their way back to the Horse and Groom where young William Ware succumbed to his wounds and died. The coroner's jury gave a verdict of murder by persons unknown. Try as I may I could find no further reference to the affair in subsequent issues of the paper. In response to my question of William Ware being responsible for supernatural appearances at the inn, the landlord answered in the negative.

The long-standing host had been plagued for several years by a phantom tippler. The spirit cupboard, to which he had the only key, was often found unlocked with a couple of drams gone from every bottle. I suggested that some member of staff obtained the key from the previous owner. The landlord informed me that this was most unlikely as he had brought his own staff with him and had changed the lock since his arrival. Very strange indeed.

A second spirit at the Horse and Groom is a kindly old lady who keeps to herself upstairs. Most of the staff in the late 1960s were on nodding acquaintance with the old lady and treated her with respect. However, the landlord's babysitters took a little time to adjust. Left alone with young children it was quite a shock to hear the old lady's footsteps as she busied herself with domestic chores upstairs. Perhaps the hustle and bustle of this popular eating house has convinced the old lady to shuffle off to a spirit's retirement home – her assistance is no longer required. She has neither been seen nor heard of for over a decade.

South Hill Park, a wonderful old building left over from the time of elegance, has experienced a number of inexplicable occurrences. In these days of less personal opulence the vast building is now owned by the local authorities and houses art rooms, a cinema, a theatre, several bars, conference rooms and a massive and attractive stair case, built by my great-grandfather George Long.

In the 1920s, Major Rickman OBE came into possession of South Hill Park. The Major inherited it from his aunt, a Mrs Haversham. Unfortunately for Rickman he also inherited a large debt. After years of trying to get on an even financial plane, the Major capitulated and shot himself in the gun room (why is this story beginning to resemble a game of Cluedo?).

For some reason the Major's shade walks the long veranda that runs at the back of the main bar. When I was a child, myself and others would rouse our scrumping companions by screaming, 'Here comes the Major!' The phantom Major has been witnessed little of late; he has no doubt been deterred by the hordes of people that flock to picnic on the vast lawns in summer.

There are other supernatural happenings that have occurred at more recent dates; among them, strange whistling noises and doors that open and shut by themselves without the slightest breeze. Both of these strange happenings occurred on a regular basis and were witnessed by security guards who also experienced regular uncanny feelings of being watched.

Jeffrey Nicholls, author of *Our Mysterious Shire*, relates a story told to him by a lady in the 1980s. Apparently she was sorting props for a local performance, which required her to move a table and cloth. She moved the table to the centre of the stage leaving the cloth folded on the floor. When she returned to the cloth she found it was only a couple of yards behind her, suspended in midair. After several seconds, it drifted downwards as if released by an unseen hand. This strange happening has been associated with a playful phantom child who seems interested in any drama that involves children. She has been witnessed standing shyly on the fringe of auditions for children. It is speculated that she wished to become part of the production and appears when there is a group involved. Incidentally, when my two daughters were in their early teens they witnessed a smiling child watching them from the staircase.

Easthampstead

Easthampstead (once the home of Shelley) has been swallowed up by Bracknell for many years and remains virtually in name only. Outside the village, up a long attractive drive stands Easthampstead Park. Once the home of Lord Downshire, this lovely old building has been metamorphosed many times. For a decade or two it was a lady's training college for potential teachers. I was a vibrant teenager in Crowthorne just 3 miles away. My best friend was the son of the Principal there. We had many happy adventures, often exaggerated, with the eighty or so young females that boarded there.

There was always the talk of the ghost; an old lady, thought to have been a cleaner, who was often witnessed by the stairs. Incidentally, the massive and intricate staircase was another of those erected by George Long my great-grandfather

For some years now, Easthampstead Park has played host to training sessions for private firms, talks, conferences, weddings, funerals and all types of receptions. I had not visited the Old Hall for many years, but recently in early 2010 I was there at a funeral. While chatting with a receptionist I chanced to say, 'How's your resident ghost?'

'Oh she is still about. She was over there by the stairs the other day,' she replied.

It's nice to know that her presence is still felt.

The Bracknell to Crowthorne Road once traversed Easthampstead in the vicinity of Dry Pond. The area has since been built on and Dry Pond no longer exists. In fact, as its name suggests it only existed when there had been sufficient rainfall. Legend has it that in the late nineteenth century one of Lord Downshire's forester's wives found her three-year-old son drowned in Dry Pond. It was accepted by generations of locals that the spirit of the distraught woman holding her still child was seen at the junction of the Crowthorne Road and a track that joined it near Dry Pond. The track is now known as Ringmead.

The Mill Pond at Easthampstead was a pleasant relaxing lake and picnic area. It is crowded on summer days with its fine walks, children's playground and cafe. There is a ghost story here concerning the mill, which has long since gone – if indeed there was ever a mill. There is little or no running water, which one would have thought necessary for grinding wheat. Studying the old maps of the area, it is evident that the wreck of an old mill is shown on early editions. It stood about a mile to the east in what is now Broadmoor Forestry (formerly Broadmoor Common). The trees are quite recently planted (about 120 years ago) and prior to that it was, as the name suggests, wild open and treeless.

Caesar's Camp is here, as is the causeway and the Devil's Highway, which is older than time and runs from London to Silchester.

But back to the pantomime. There was once a miller at Easthampstead in the early eighteenth century. The miller was a prosperous but belligerent and mean man. One freezing winter his poor neighbours were starving and begged him for food. Like a true pantomime villain, the miller refused, holding out for a better price from town.

One freezing night the miller was awakened by a knock on his door. Angrily, he opened his door to see a starving man in rags standing on the doorstep. He begged the miller desperately for food.

'Be off,' said the miller, or words to that effect. 'I shall set the dogs on you.'

In the morning the miller discovered the body of the ragged man and from that day onwards all went wrong for the miller. His crops failed, his cattle died, his millstones cracked – all as if by magic. That's not all; his land flooded and his wife went off with a computer salesman. His daughter married an income tax inspector and his son became a Spurs supporter. The final straw was when he began to be haunted by the man in rags who the miller had cruelly ignored. The miller took to the roads, begging for a living. All the cottagers shut their doors to him; his mill was burnt to the ground and his son-in-law, the tax inspector, took over his fields. Still, in Broadmoor's deepest forestry, on dark nights, the noise of running footsteps and the sound of a man puffing and crying can be heard. If you wait one more minute you may catch sight of a ragged beggar giving chase.

There was once a house at Caesar's Camp. I remember it well. It had a deep well, which went down so far it was scary to look down. In those days, the late 1950s and early 1960s, the house had been left derelict. It was finally demolished and the well filled in.

Once again, I am indebted to Angus Macnaughten, who tells of a lady who contacted him. She lived in the house at Caesar's Camp during the Second World War, at a time when troops used to use it as a training ground before being sent to Europe. One night the lady was awakened by the sounds of marching and singing soldiers – not an unusual event by day, but unique by night. The lady stood at the door to watch the march past. She heard it but she never saw it. The sound continued but there was no one insight.

Angus's correspondent went on to mention a second and third story. I gained more interest as I read on. Apparently, the first lady had a sister who lived with her and her son in the cottage. One night the sister awoke to find a man standing by her bed. The man was tall with strikingly ugly features and red hair. She was terrified but managed to call out, 'What do you want?' Her sister came to her assistance, but the man turned and literally vanished. The correspondent went on to say that after her sister had left to live elsewhere, she remained in the cottage with her son, a boy of fourteen years.

One day the boy rushed into the house telling his mother to bolt the door as there was a strange man approaching with his face all screwed up. His mother ran upstairs but could see nothing but an empty road from the window.

I am not a great believer in coincidence, but here is a very strange rejoinder to the above. In the early 1960s a group of us teenagers were playing around on the 'Rec' (recreation ground). Among us was a special friend of mine, a small lad who we should call Dooley. For some unknown reason the talk turned to ghosts. Stories were getting more exaggerated and less believable by the minute. Finally there was a pause in the conversation and Dooley quietly stated, 'I saw a ghost once, a man with a terribly mutilated face.'

Easthampstead Park, home of the haunted staircase.

The other lads suddenly burst into action, jumping about and pointing at the small lad, shouting in chorus, 'Dooley's seen a ghostie.' In the face of such ridicule Dooley could not be induced to speak further on the subject. About three or four years later when Dooley was firmly entrenched in the army, I was chatting to my father and his name cropped up. During the conversation my father informed me that Dooley had spent his childhood staying with his old aunt at the cottage at Caesar's Camp.

Lastly at Easthampstead, surrounded by a massive housing estate, is a new pub, partly housed in an old building. It has maintained its original name of Peacocks Farm. As it was just a stones throw from the aforementioned Easthampstead Park, my friend and I spent days mooching about the area. It is accepted by the locals that the old place was haunted – by whom or what I have never discovered. Recently, in my guise as a *Wokingham Times* columnist, I called at the inn for a drink. I enquired, 'Is the old place still haunted?' The

The haunted Berystede
Hotel, Sunninghill.

landlord replied that there was something very strange in the adjacent farmhouse where he was staying.

Sunninghill

The structure of Sunninghill has altered little in the previous centuries; the buildings, mostly Georgian seem to remain stoic and solid. There were reports of hauntings in one particular building in the 1960s. The spectre, a middle-aged woman, was often observed crossing the drawing-room and exiting through a solid wall. A lady who lived in the house for many years reported several strange experiences. Having retired for the night, she remained sleepless and so she decided to return to the drawing room to retrieve a book. On entering she was surprised, nay shocked, to see a woman who appeared solid with her hands held as if holding a book. The ghostly lady, who incidentally was attired in modern clothes, simply turned and disappeared. Several years later, in the Midlands, this lady was staying with friends. She instantly recognized another guest there as the lady she had seen in her front room. Naturally enough the other guest denied all knowledge of the house and ever visiting it.

I am fond of the Berystede Hotel at Sunninghill. There is a certain romantic dignity about the place, which is so difficult to find in this day and age. The hotel, a large and attractive building, was erected on the site of an old house, once home of the Standish family; it's a very opulent and impressive building indeed. On the morning of 27 October 1886, this palatial mansion caught fire. In a short time it was literally razed to the ground. Originally it was believed that everyone had survived, but later the charred remains of Eliza Kleineger, Mrs Standish's French maid, were discovered at the bottom of the servant's staircase.

Over the decades this mature lady had collected jewels and trinkets from various employers. Although it is thought she had originally escaped the blaze it is also surmised that she returned for her priceless baubles. She had then being trapped by blazing timbers and had finally expired through smoke inhalation. When the old house was rebuilt as a swish hotel, staff soon found that Eliza was loath to leave her post. The spectre is often observed under the central gable where the original servant's staircase used to be. She appears, small, withered and always worrying. With a deep look of apprehension on her face, the little French maid seems indecisive as to whether she should brave the flames or not.

9

Ascot

NEVER let people tell you that Bramshott in Hants or Pluckley in Kent is Britain's most haunted village. Without doubt, there are more spirits residing in Berkshire's Royal Ascot than anywhere else in the British Isles – so many in fact that I must be brief.

Where the winding A329 from Ascot to Virginia Waters is at its darkest and narrowest, one could be unlucky enough to meet Ascot's phantom policeman. When approached by car he is just a tall shadowy figure walking towards Virginia Waters. Cars have been known to narrowly miss him and as the motorist turns to see if he has caused any injury he notices, with mounting alarm and terror, that above the policeman's high collared tunic and underneath his high shiny hat, is the most terribly mutilated face imaginable. There are reports of drivers too terrified to continue their journey and others who report their sightings to local police stations.

Who is this terribly disfigured officer of the law? Was he attacked and badly beaten? Did he die in an accident? Was he a local officer born with these terrible features?

The answer to all these questions is no. There is no record of a policeman being murdered or maliciously attacked here, neither is there any record of an officer with natural disfigurements. This poor spectre must continue his lonely, endless patrol. I have my own ideas about him, which I shall go into later in the book.

A private house in Ascot in the mid-1970s experienced some unusual, if not unique, poltergeist activity. It was unusual because it featured a private car with a mind of its own. Despite the family's night watches, their saloon managed to shift itself nearly every night for several weeks. Apart from avoiding nocturnal scrutiny, the car had little regard for gravel drives and locked doors. What was most unusual was that the car moved in a sideways direction, usually about 10ft. These strange events were soon to attract the attention of the local media, but it was only considered newsworthy for a limited time. As far as I know, the mystery was never solved.

Here's a lovely little Ascot ghost story supplied by a charismatic and pleasant person. In 1930 Wilfred Hyde White had a strange experience at Ascot races. Wilfred was walking the course with a friend a week prior to Royal Ascot. Here the famous actor must have experienced what he called afterwards a time slip. Suddenly he could hear a throng of people; market traders shouted their wares, women laughed, men joked and children indulged in exciting chatter. One voice of a child closer to hand stated that the Queen was not wearing her crown. Just as distinctly, a voice over the sound system announced the first, second and third place positions in the half past three race. It also stated that a treble would pay £168 for a £1 bet.

Wilfred stood transfixed for what he described as approximately two minutes. Considering the matter afterwards he was struck with the idea that he had been jilted back to Victoria's reign. By now, fascinated by the whole affair, he worked meticulously through ancient programmes, but nowhere could he find a past meeting where the three named horses had taken the positions in any race attended by royals, or in any race at all for that matter.

Much later it dawned on Wilfred that he may just as well have been swept forward in time as backward. He supported this prognosis when he discovered that the sound system had only been installed shortly before Elizabeth II's succession to the throne. Could the Queen mentioned be Elizabeth rather than Victoria? Wilfred Hyde White keenly scoured the Ascot race cards for many years, but sadly the listed horses never appeared – well they haven't as yet anyway.

It would be impossible to write on supernatural occurrences at Ascot without mentioning Angus Macnaughten. I am indebted to Angus for the following creepy little gem. It tells of mild poltergeist activity at a private house in Fernbank Road. In his book *Windsor Ghosts and Berkshire Hauntings*, Angus points out that the house was occupied by a family of four; father, mother and two very young boys. It has been fairly well accepted over the years that poltergeist activity is attracted by youngsters. It seems that in some way they create, unconsciously, an unknown form of static electricity that is powerful enough to move or otherwise affect inanimate objects, and through some totally unscientific reason, albeit coincidental, the activity is strongest where teenagers, particularly girls, are present. Could there be an association with the common traumas that face young people between the ages of twelve and twenty?

The Fernbank Road case was pretty much run of the mill: articles were thrown about the house, doors opened and closed, lights turn themselves off and on, cars moved and trembled and a host of other minor and annoying occurrences developed. Angus informs that a wooden figure from Nigeria shouldered the blame, which seems quite illogical. However, when it was removed over the Christmas holidays things improved immeasurably, only to return with increased verve when the figure was replaced.

I must mention very briefly a couple more manifestations that Angus's book brought to my notice. One is mistress at a renowned Ascot girl's school who committed suicide on the premises and is said to haunt that part of the building.

The second, slightly better known, is Admiral Sullivan, a retired gentleman who inhabited a house near the racecourse. Before he died it was the Admiral's want to stand at a bay window observing all with his telescope. The old gentleman's demise seems not to have terminated his habits; his shade continued to study the surrounding terrain and apparently on a sunny day the glint of his telescope might catch your eye.

Jeff Nicholls, in his book *Our Mysterious Shire*, first informed me of Huntingdon. Huntingdon was erected in 1898 and was all but razed to the ground in 1977. The top floor was badly damaged; it was probably beneficial that the house was derelict at the time and there was no chance of human casualties. Some hours after the blaze was extinguished, at

time Huntsman to Queen Anne. Charles was thrown from his horse in 1792 and died of a broken neck. An unlikely legend states that while a portrait of Davies remains in the house, all will be well. However, should it be removed from the premises the spectre of Davies, complete with his fractured neck lolling on the shoulders and his tongue protruding from his spectral mouth, will walk the corridors until it is returned.

Where the Bracknell to Virginia Water Road crosses the Windsor Road in the vicinity of Heatherwood and Ascot Racecourse there is a now a massive roundabout. It was once a mere crossroads and on the Bracknell / Windsor Road corner stood the Royal Ascot Hotel. It was rather dilapidated in the 1960s when I dropped in for an occasional drink. Rumour had it that a famous racehorse, whose name had been forgotten in the mists of time, was buried under the lawn in front of the hotel. Legend stated that each year on the date of the horse's demise, the spectral horse would arise through the earth and canter around the course. The spectral animal has not surfaced for a number of years now and the Royal Ascot Hotel is long gone. The site is now covered by the most luxurious and expensive block of apartments, arguably in the country. Is it any wonder the poor old horse fails to surface? Imagine trying to push your way through that lot.

A well-known and better authenticated ghost here is reputedly a nun. What seems strange is her choice of venue; the Ascot Working Men's Club, which has been situated in the High Street for many decades.

3 o'clock the following morning, a fire officer returned to dampen down. The officer had inspected the building and was on his way out when he noticed a little old lady. In Jeff's book she is described as being attired in a long black dress and black boots, with her bonnet tied under her chin. As the old lady descended the stairs, the officer, thinking her a concerned neighbour enquired, 'Can I help you? What are you doing here?'

The fire officer's enquiries were ignored and he stated that within seconds of approaching the old lady to ask her to leave, she disappeared. Checking all the available rooms for her whereabouts was futile – she was gone. Who she was and where she went to has been open to conjecture for years. Huntingdon has since been demolished.

The next tale is very old and, to be truthful, more legend than supernatural. A good stones throw from the site of Huntingdon on the Windsor Road is Old Huntsman's House. The house is reputedly haunted by Charles Davies, a previous owner and one-

A spate of unusual happenings have been reported, such as beer taps turning themselves off, gaming machines acting suspiciously, cupboard doors opening and closing of their own volition and other general mild poltergeist behaviour.

Why a nun? If it is a nun, why haunt a drinking and gambling establishment? Would it be too fanciful to suggest that she appears to give warning to people she incorrectly judges as decadent? Visiting here back in the 1970s, I made several lighthearted enquiries as to how they knew their phantom visitor was a nun. I was told that on the several occasions when she had materialised, she was attired in long flowing robes and wimple.

What of the surroundings? There have been a number of monasteries, priories and nunneries scattered around the Ascot area over the centuries; our lady could have been connected to any one of them. Also, there are several Catholic schools ruled by ladies similarly attired to the club's spectral visitor. Like many ghost stories, this one must remain a mystery. It has been suggested to me that the spectre is that of a novice drowned in Englemere Pond in the 1920s. At the moment I can trace no record of this, so for the want of more evidence I shall have 'nun' of it for the time being anyway!

Within the last half a century, I have covered over 4,000 supposedly haunted sites, delivered sixteen volumes covering the subject to a very patient readership and slept in over sixty alleged haunted bedrooms. But there are still places that intrigue me, which up to now I have not had the opportunity to explore. No less than seven such sites are in Ascot. One is Ascot Priory of which tales of ghostly moanings and possible prayers abound.

Another is Ascot Place, a very private place indeed. I will admit to a tingle of jealousy toward those who have been permitted to see its fine Gothic follies. I am told that there is a fine grotto here, rivalling the one at Margate which is well known to me. There are other follies here in the shape of a Gothic seat and a Dry Bridge. I am informed that there is a tunnel joining two gardens with a bas-relief woman's countenance guarding the west entrance.

The grandson of an old gardener here tells me that there are eerie gibbering sounds that exude from the tunnel. Which came first I wonder? The ghostly eerie gibberings or the two small statues of apes that guard the east end of the tunnel?

10

Warfield

The Plough and Harrow

An inn that seems to be surviving all the nearly insurmountable drawbacks of the last few years is the Plough and Harrow. There is a colourful ghost story here. The venue is the car park and road outside rather than the pub itself.

The story originates at Warfield Park, once a massive and dominant feature of the area. It has been demolished for many years now and the grounds are currently a vast caravan park. In the 1870s the park was owned and dominated by the less than popular Lord Ormanthwaite. He was married to the lovely and refined Lady Emily, daughter of the Duke of Beaufort. Unlike her husband, she was a philanthropic lady, known for her charitable deeds in the area and was well liked indeed.

Lady Emily, it was rumoured, was regularly beaten by her husband. While she was the soul of discretion, her husband's violent behaviour soon became known to the villagers and one day, while she was practising her charitable work in Warfield, it was noticed that she was badly bruised. The villagers decided the best way to protect her was by giving his Lordship an exhibition of canning. Canning involved a large group of people meeting outside the Plough and Harrow, armed with anything that would make a loud noise. Men, women and children produced pots and pans, whistles, pipes, buckets and spades.

When the ragged orchestra was complete it marched towards Warfield Park making the loudest and most horrendous din. On reaching its destination the crowd made a non-stop commotion all night, thereby showing its umbrage at Lord Ormanthwaite's behaviour towards his wife. The good Lord could do little more than take the names of the leading offenders.

These events took place on 28 October 1874. Ever since then hardy ghost-hunters take a watch by the Plough and Harrow, because legend dictates that there is a ghostly re-enactment of the proceedings on its anniversary each year. There were several reports in the 1930s that claimed to have met with some success.

There is another story attached to the same incident, which was related to me in the 1960s by an inhabitant of Warfield who claimed that his father was one of the original marchers. My informant told me that there was a small crippled boy in the village who had a badly clubbed foot. The lad's whole ambition in life was to become a soldier; an ambition that his deformed foot would obviously prohibit.

Lady Emily, hearing of the lad's problem, had made for him a specially tailored scarlet uniform of military style. She also provided him with a drum. These were his most prized possessions other than a pet monkey, a present given to him from his recently demised soldiering father. It is the spirit of the young drummer boy with his monkey that is believed to lead the ghostly throng, as he did in life so many years ago. Having checked with other ancient villagers in the 1960s I found that they concurred with the story. They also pointed out that there was once a pub in Warfield named the Drum and Monkey in honour of the little soldier.

Before leaving Warfield Park I must mention Rachel. Warfield Park was destroyed by fire in 1766 and a new house (also now gone) was built on this site, constructed by Colonel John Walsh. Walsh was a ladies man, a man of many mistresses. One such lady was Rachel. Unfortunately, Rachel thought herself to be Walsh's only mistress and on discovering that she was one of many, she was overcome with grief and drowned herself in an ornamental lake. Thereafter it was known as Rachel's Lake. Sightings of Rachel's shade have been unusually consistent. A lady in a Jacobean style dress has appeared crossing the main drive on numerous occasions. Motorists are the worst affected, as the spectre seems to come from nowhere, causing them to brake sharply. Apparently, on several occasions they are not able to break sharply enough and have damaged their vehicles by swerving off of the road.

Anybody who has visited Warfield lately will notice that several vast estates have been built. I am pleased to say that the council are still in touch with romance and tradition though: a new road is aptly named Rachel's Lake View.

The Yorkshire Rose

About 100 yards along the Forest Road from the Plough and Harrow stands the Yorkshire Rose, a restaurant and bar. The building is very old, but I believe the licence was acquired comparatively recently. Prior to that, it was a gentile tea and scone establishment. Going back even further, the Yorkshire Rose, suspected to be nearly 300 years old, was itself built on a far older site; nearby Priory Lane gives us a clue.

The Yorkshire Rose was once a staging post, manned by monks who provided sustenance to travellers brave enough to attempt the notorious Forest Road between Windsor and Reading. It is little surprise that the resident ghost is a figure dressed in black robes, who flits speedily across the old tea room. It is possible that the spirit has moved on now, because there have been no reports of him for over thirty years. This, however, does not completely exempt the building of all supernatural

interest. Paper cups and plates often develop a will of their own and a low, nearly inaudible chanting has been heard by staff. They describe the chanting as awakening a friendly benign feeling, rather than one of fear and malevolence.

Quelm Lane

Unusual name for a lane, Quelm Lane. Years ago it was almost unknown. I used to get to it by turning off Newell Green into Watersplash Lane and turning left before reaching the ford. Quelm Lane was popular with dog walkers, if not with dogs. That's right, our canine friends were much adverse to walking up it.

A well-known old local story relates that Quelm Lane was frequented by a man on a very large horse who kidnapped children. He flung them across the back of his massive black stallion and they were never seen again. Obviously this was a tale to scare children into not staying out too late. There are plenty of accounts similar to this one all over the country.

I dealt with one such tale in a book, *I'll be Hanged* many years ago. People in north-west Berkshire used to threaten their children with it, 'Come in, or old Danny Grimshaw will get you.' The rumour was that old Danny was a cannibal who boiled children alive before eating them. In actuality old Danny, a man in his early twenties, had accidentally killed his baby son with boiling water. At his trial the judge, in his summing up, stated that with such a tiny amount of circumstantial evidence it would be very difficult to find him guilty. The jury, terrified of public opinion, were having none of it. Danny was convicted and hanged; at least there was a modicum of history attached to this story.

As far as the horse and rider story is concerned there is nothing at all. I was sure that even years ago in rural Berkshire, one missing child at least would be recorded, but there are no such records. It has been suggested to me that the horse and rider are ghosts. Mind you, it would be difficult for a shade to lift a child, place it across the back of a ghostly horse and spirit it away. Nonetheless, there was always a very strange feeling in Quelm Lane and I for one am a great believer in canine intuition where ghosts are concerned. What ever was in Quelm Lane it has been nudged out by a recent massive building programme. The eerie feeling seems to have disappeared. Incidentally, 'quelm' is the old English word for the gallows and Quelm Lane was known as Hangman's Lane.

11

Winkfield

THE Royal Foresters, sadly now no more, was a popular hostelry on the famous Drift Road. There was always a warm old atmosphere at the Foresters. When it turned into a cider house there was a plethora of strange experiences. The pity is that so few were recorded. There are unsubstantiated tales of a spectral horse invading the garden and a man with a soundless French horn standing by the gate. All is conjecture, nothing is authenticated.

Angus Macnaughten again tells us of a private house near the Foresters that was haunted by a lady with a mop cap, obviously a servant from the past. It is a pity that her more modern counterparts found her difficult to live with, as they regularly gave in their notice. The same house has a pond at the side, which horses refuse to pass after dusk.

A nearby house was once owned by two quarrelsome brothers; they often argued and at one stage fought a duel. However, neither brother received a fatal blow and things seemed to quieten down. But it wasn't long before a dead brother then surfaced from the pond. Murder or accidental death? No one knows. But the drowned brother's shade, wringing wet, was witnessed for some years after the event.

The Herne's Oak

Herne's exploits have been related in dozens of books, including one of my own. The happenings at the Herne's Oak pub, obviously named after the overworked phantom-hunter, are far less exciting. It seems that from time to time on a summer's evening the sound of an invisible horse passes the inn. It is thought to be the ghost of a stallion that escaped from a nearby circus's winter quarters and was struck and killed by a lorry. Why a horse that was killed on a winter's day should frequent a summer evening is not easily explained.

The White Hart

The White Hart is probably the oldest and most attractive pub in an area literally inundated with old and attractive pubs. The White Hart is reputed to be partly thirteenth century. It did not gain a licence to sell beer until as late as 1593. The original name was the Old Courthouse, and in all probability it acted as the local Verderers' Court. This would fit in with the local ghost story that a weeping man lost his land holdings after cheating

on his commoner's rights. This very fanciful story goes that he fled the court and ran to the church opposite, where he took his own life. We are not informed as to how. The poor man's shade has not been seen for over seventy years, if indeed it ever was.

Ye Olde Hatchet

Ye Olde Hatchet is another ancient and attractive inn residing in the Winkfield area. As with many others it began its life as a woodsman's cottage, in fact two adjacent cottages. Foresters in olden days brewed their own ale to save a trip into town. It would then be sold to neighbours, and in this way the country pub was born. The Hatchet boasts an old brass engine, but of more interest to us is the courtyard, now the car park. It was once used to host bare knuckle fighting. A bruiser is thought to have died in a bout here, not as unusual an occurrence, as you may expect. He is now reputed to haunt the car park, but once again this is a spirit that has not shown itself for over fifty years.

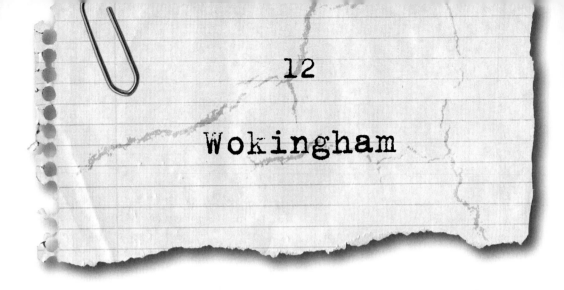

12

Wokingham

ET'S start with Claude Duval. It is reported by people unknown that the romantic French Highwayman had a house in Wokingham and that the sound of his horse's hooves can be heard in Rose Street. There is no record of the house, but a lady of nearly the same name was said to be his aunt. The relationship is nearly as unlikely as the ghostly sounds.

I heard sometime ago, that a gentleman who had an older house in Finchampstead Road was frequently disturbed by an old gentleman in a frock coat sitting on his bed. The trouble is that the reports were in 1960, now half a century ago.

In 1979, local newspapers reported that an office block in Wokingham was haunted. On several occasions, a cleaner working in the typist pool, saw a figure in the corner of her eye that would disappear when she turned to look at it. Also, at about this time, two window cleaners reported seeing strange sights behind them from the reflections in the windows. The original cleaner had a slightly more worrying experience when, as she travelled down in the lift, she felt a resounding smack across her bottom.

Frog Hall in Frog Hall Drive, opposite the Three Frogs, was reputed to be haunted.

This once Queen Anne-style house was much altered prior to becoming flats. One ghost here is an elderly gentleman in morning attire; another is a lady playing a spinet. Whether it is either of these friendly ghosts or perhaps a separate spirit that was responsible for the mild poltergeist activity here is open to speculation.

Tom Lethbridge, a thorough and tireless investigator of the supernatural, lived in Wokingham in the early 1950s. As a teenager I had the privilege to meet him. Tom went on to far greater things and always looked at the unknown through imaginative and logical eyes. He was a great believer in natural atmosphere causing supernatural incidents.

It was a sunny day in Bigwood, Wokingham when Tom and his mother were suddenly engulfed in a deep form of depression; a strangely frightening gloom and despair. As the pair walked on, the atmosphere lightened and then completely lifted. Three days later the body of a missing suicide was discovered very close to the park where Tom and his mother had felt the depression.

In the mid-1950s through to the early 1960s my sister and my cousin, Jennifer, occasionally attended Wokingham County Girls School (the Holt). There had been many stories of there being an underground passage here to the Town Hall, a distance of over half a mile. With the rumours of the passageway came more rumours of uncanny noises and ghosts, but as far as I know nothing supernatural was ever discovered. I made enquiries later on and was informed of various outcomes. Some ex-pupils told me that the passage was never discovered; others maintained that it was traced and then blocked.

Supposedly a haunted school that no longer exists once stood on Nine Mile Ride just south of Wokingham. It was a boarding and day school to young boys. Now demolished, it is the site of numerous houses, but it once stood empty and alone. As a part-time job my late wife often cleaned there and I visited on many occasions. The place certainly had an eerie atmosphere, far deeper than that which usually accompanies old empty buildings.

My daughters, who were very young at the time, claimed to have seen the ghost of an old lady there. Possibly it was a domestic worker who was unwilling to leave the building. After putting the story down to overactive juvenile imaginations, I contacted other people who had once been employed there. Several had seen the old lady and had said nothing for fear of ridicule.

Wokingham also has its fair share of haunted pubs; when I was in my teens there used to be thirty-four licensed premises in town. Despite trade restrictions, smoking bans and a whole host of disadvantages, nearly thirty establishments still remain. Down by the station the Three Brewers, named after the town's three breweries, has reported mild poltergeist activity over the years. It was once run by friends of mine who regularly reported things that went bump in the night. I wonder what supernatural activity there is in more recent times.

Up in the centre of town, in Rose Street is the Metropolitan, the last to remain of some eight pubs that flourished in the street before the Second World War. The Metropolitan certainly had a haunted chair; well, not so much haunted as unlucky. It was rumoured that patrons who sat on it would often not have long for this world. I believe and trust that it has been destroyed.

On a nearby corner stands The Ship, one of the most popular hostelries in the town. In 1970 the *Wokingham Times* interviewed the landlord, who insisted the place was haunted. Weird noises were reported from an alcove in a small room above the patio. The landlord insisted that there were no water pipes nearby, which are often blamed the supernatural sounds.

There were more uncanny reports in 1989. I spoke to a relief manager who was in *situ* at the time and stated that now the noises came from the cellar. They included the sound of a table or stalls being dragged across the floor and a continual rattling of pots and pans of their own volition. The relief manager's dog resolutely refused to enter various rooms including the cellar.

Towards Bracknell, set in immaculate grounds, is a large hotel. It was once a Catholic girl's school; prior to that it was nunnery. With this building's history it is little surprise that it is haunted by one of the country's spectral nuns. This lady has been witnessed strolling across the magnificent lawns. The nun is described as being as benign and serene as her surroundings.

Back into town we find the New Rose Inn, once the Olde Rose Inne and shortly to become a Café Rouge. It is there that the poets Dean Swift, Alexander Pope and John Gay wrote verses to Molly Mogg, the landlord's beautiful daughter. When the Olde Rose Inne was renovated several years ago, the company asked for suggestions for a new name. Personally I thought we should honour three famous local poets and suggested the

The Olde Rose Inne, Wokingham.

Gay Swift Pope. Unfortunately, it wasn't accepted, although I'm sure it was more imaginative than the New Rose.

The resident ghost here is a serving girl, who in the nineteenth century was impregnated by the then-time equivalent of a travelling salesman. He promised to stand by her, but in reality took to the road, never to seen again.

In a fit of depression she hanged herself from a tree in the garden. The hapless spirit has been linked to three fires at the Rose in the 1960s and 1970s. Poor girl, did she not have enough trouble? Why should a ghost, content with walking corridors for 150 years, suddenly turn into a pyromaniac? It's a mystery.

For many years I ran a small removals business and came across many landlords in my work. One, a personal friend of mine, moved into the Lord Raglan. After he had been in for a couple of weeks the new landlord discovered a bedroom with a very malevolent atmosphere. He asked me if I should like to sleep there to feel it for myself.

I have slept in many supposedly haunted rooms, usually fortified and accompanied by my pal Johnnie Walker I admit. Several dates were made but something always seemed to postpone the fateful night. Later I returned from abroad to find my friend had moved to a pub some distance away.

Arborfield

Let us start with the notorious Arborfield witch. The notorious witch she might well be, but her name is unknown. All we know is that she was a farmer's wife from the Reading Road. The witch was suspected of, and blamed for, much of the mischief in the area and often took the form of a black cat that spirited sheep and cows, which in turn caused their milk to curdle. The witch also turned placid dogs mad and destroyed all the crops with torrents of rain. Worst of all, she caused the wind to blow the wigs off the heads of local dignitaries.

Something had to be done, so some of the stronger men of the village banded together and seized her, bound her and threw her into a pond to drown. Apparently this was not enough, the witch may have been dead, but her spirit ascended and descended into the pond at regular intervals. The village elders decided that the witch's (presumably rotting) body had to be kept at the bottom of the pond, so a vast stone was procured and placed against the witch's corpse, and that was the end of the Arborfield witch.

Well no, not quite. Just after the Second World War the powers that be decided that there was no longer a need for a village pond and so workmen drained it. When it was dry they discovered a massive white stone. Intrigued, they decided to lift it, but before this was possible the locals, who even in 1948 were still steeped in superstition, refused to have it moved. They got their way and the area was grassed over, the stone still in place.

Even that was not quite the end. When I worked for a firm of landscape gardeners in the late 1990s they had much trouble cutting the grass at the scene. Mowers, temperamental things at the best of times, packed up for no apparent reason and even large industrial machines were problematic in the area. The local paper, the *Wokingham Times*, got wind of it and approached me. I could tell them no more than is written above.

Saint Bartholomew's Church at Arborfield is a strange old place and some very mysterious happenings have occurred there.

The site of a witch's entombment in Arborfield.

St Bartholomew's Church, Arborfield.

Horse accident in Barkham.

On 3 February 1995, the *Wokingham Times* reported that a 100-year-old corpse had been found smouldering in a family crypt. The vicar had discovered the strange phenomena on Saturday lunchtime when he saw smoke rising from the Hargrave family crypt. The fire brigade was called and carried the skeleton outside on the coffin lid. The crypt had been interfered with before and the human remains had remained on top of the coffin ever since. The whole episode was played down and was thought to have been a child's prank.

The previous skulduggery had occurred in 1963 when the coffin had been smashed and the family vault sacked. Imaginative ideas at the time included one that suggested the vault had hidden some of the proceeds from The Great Train Robbery. This theory was partially endorsed by the gardener's wife, who had heard lorries nearby on the night.

Ten years later there were more disturbances. Firstly a skull was found in the churchyard. It was soon realised that the crypt had been vandalised; skeletons and separate bones lay in profusion. Theories of black magic and the occult surfaced once again. When the coffins were re-shelved it was noticed that one was missing. It is now assumed without a slither of evidence that

money had been concealed in the coffin ten years previously and then recovered. The trail went dead until the 1995 experience and nothing amiss has happened since.

Arborfield's spectral bride could be from an Edgar Allan Poe poem, or out of a B film from Hammer House of Horrors couldn't it? An old church stands within the grounds of Arborfield Hall. The Hall itself doesn't stand at all; it was demolished many years ago. Reports of the spectral bride in a long white flowing dress have occasionally surfaced here. She is very distressed and stands under a yew tree on New Year's Eve. She is waiting for her lover, for she is to be married the following day to a romantic young gardener who is employed at the Hall. She waits in vain, but she catches her breath when a figure approaches. Alas, not the figure of her lover. No, it is the fat, bloated, ugly butler from the Hall. Mad with jealousy, he puts her to death (by what means we are not informed). Neither are we are informed as to what happens to the jealous butler after his murderous act. The murdered maid returns as a ghost. Of the handsome young lover nothing is known. In some accounts he has already been slain and is pushing up the daisies in one of his own flowerbeds. That's right, the butler did it!

Barkham

Barkham was a superb little village, but now it has all but been engulfed by Wokingham. A headless soldier mounted on a horse rises from the old Rectory Marsh and noiselessly canters along the Barkham Road to Barkham Hill, where he promptly disappears. Barkham has a second headless ghost too, also mounted on a horse. A white, headless lady in flowing garments rides a black horse from a similar direction. An accident between the two could be fatal.

The third supernatural being at Barkham is not really a ghost in the accepted sense of the word; she was a witch who dwelt in Sandy Lane. She was always at odds with the local agisters (local men who made sure that common land was parcelled out fairly for cattle grazing). Agisters Lane runs parallel with Sandy Lane and here, a deep throbbing noise, which scares dogs, is thought to come from the witch.

Bearwood

Bearwood was once the home of John Walter, the founder of *The Times* newspaper. There was a succession of John Walters, as fathers passed the name to sons, each adding or changing part of their magnificent old building. On Christmas Eve in 1870, John the fourth was drowned trying to save his younger brother and cousin from the lake. They had fallen through the ice while skating. I have always found the lake a very eerie place; possibly not so much anymore, now that it is surrounded by golf clubs and other venues of varying entertainments.

So what haunts Bearwood? One of those who perished in the lake? Apparently not. It is the house, a long-time home of the Royal Merchant Navy School, that is haunted – strangely by a red dwarf. Nobody has the slightest idea who he was and what connection he had with the building though. He has been seen on the stairs and various other places.

Bearwood School, home of a ghostly dwarf.

Monks Alley,
Binfield.

Stag and Hounds, Binfield.

Binfield

The Stag and Hounds stands on Forest Road; once a track that ran the length of Windsor Forest. It was thought to have been a fourteenth-century hunting lodge that was transformed into an inn in 1727. It is said that Queen Elizabeth first stayed here en route to Windsor. What is without doubt is that William Cobbett, of *Rural Rides* fame, stayed here in the 1820s; there is evidence that he complimented the breakfast when he stayed.

When investigating *Final Commitment*, my third book on Berkshire murderers, I came across a couple of newspapers that mentioned Rosa Rose. In December 1869 Rosa Rose took her very young child, a boy named Johnny, from where she stayed in Church Street, Reading to her mothers in Warfield. She walked the distance in pouring rain, although she had more than sufficient funds for the coach journey. A bedraggled Rosa, complete with child, stopped for liquid refreshment at the Stag and Hounds, possibly to gain courage before meeting her mother, who lived half a mile away in Warfield.

Her mother was very much opposed to Rosa's second mistake – Johnny being her second illegitimate child and it is thought that Rosa was turned away. She and Johnny were exhausted and lay down to rest in a wood near the Stag and Hounds. According to Rosa they slept in spite of the deluge. When she awoke she discovered Johnny dead, in all probability he had drowned. Reports differ, but it is believed that Rosa carried the tiny body all the way back to Reading. She was arrested, but the charges were finally dropped and Rosa walked free. According to public opinion, Rosa was a very lucky lady. Was Johnny murdered? We will never know.

So who haunts the Stag and Hounds? Is it Rosa? Little Johnny? No, the seldom seen spectre here is an Ostler who hanged him-self in the stables, which is now part of the dining area.

Some ten years ago I was writing accounts of ghost stories in the *Wokingham Times*. At the same time I was working at Tesco's. One day I was chatting to a young lady who was also employed there; she had read several of my columns and related a story of her own. She informed me that she and half a dozen other youngsters were returning after a night out. Their route occasioned them to drive down Monks Alley at Binfield. The car's headlights suddenly lit up a cowled figure. Judging by the attire it was assumed to be a monk. As they neared the crouching, humped figure it turned towards the light, revealing a hideously deformed face; the expression was one of evil and hatred. So intimidated were the party that the three men got out and walked beside the car as the three girls remained inside. The apparition seemed to recoil and then it disappeared.

Try as I may, I can find no torturous death or mutilations attached to Monks Alley, but obviously the very name suggests that there were some of the monastic type dwelling there in the past. Having read my accounts, a lady wrote to me on the subject. She stated that when she took her large dog for a walk down Monks Alley, he would stand at a junction near Binfield House with his tail between his legs, hackles raised and physically shivering.

There are several very old houses in the area, some reputed to have subterranean passages. Whether or not this has any bearing on the strange incidents I do not know, but I am a great believer in the very developed sense of our canine friends.

Embrook

There are ghosts that have been witnessed at Embrook as recently as the turn of the twenty-first century. Back then a woman walking her dog in Cantley Park witnessed a striking looking lady in Victorian attire – a dark full-length dress with a tight waistband. She was described as fairly attractive with long hair worn in a bun at the back. The lady was thin, and her age was thought to be between the late thirties and early forties. The witness went on to describe the gaunt spectre as a lady who looked as if she was intent on a mission, moving absorbedly, as if meandering between trees. This is strange, as Cantley Park is now open fields, but was it always? Probably not.

The lady who reported the spectre described her as scary, probably because it was her first experience of the supernatural. Apart from her intensity the spirit seemed quite benign. After some twenty seconds the lady disappeared into what is a deep depression in the ground. The witness was intrigued and phoned the Cantley House Hotel, which stands adjacent to the Park, to enquire if there had been other reports of the Victorian lady. But there had been no other reports or sightings. Not to be put off, she contacted the *Wokingham Times*; as a result I too was contacted. I phoned the lady and had no doubt whatsoever that this was an authentic case. But there was still much to discover. I had heard reports of people getting indescribable feelings of depression there, but these reports were decades ago.

Cantley Park is now home to football pitches, car boot sales and a restaurant and bar – all pastimes far too modern to be conducive with the supernatural. That the witness had seen the shade of a lady I am certain, but as I could add nothing more, here this story should have rested.

But it didn't. Long have the old sages in their cups, spoken of the ghostly headless horseman at Bill Hill. So when a gentleman phoned me saying he wanted to talk of the ghost in the area I was ready for the worst. I was pleasantly surprised. The gentleman that phoned informed me that his grandmother had been a domestic at Bill Hill House (sadly no longer there). Apparently, in Victorian times a gentleman of the house had murdered a serving girl that he had impregnated. There was a tale of an indelible bloodstain in a room that the staff refused to go into after dark. Old maps of the place clearly show that prior to the dividing of the property, the dell, near the children's playground where the spooky Victorian lady disappeared, is as close to Bill Hill as it is to Cantley House. One must make of that what one will.

I was also contacted by a gentleman from Embrook who complained of mild poltergeist activity. It was the usual type of thing; kettles that turned themselves on and cups that exploded inside cupboards. To look at this gentleman's modern abode in a small charming estate, one would have thought it to be the last place a poltergeist would have selected as its residence. However, I have no doubt whatsoever of the gentleman's sincerity. He went on to inform me of a couple he had seen while walking his dog, Billy, in a nearby park. The gentleman noticed some 80 yards away a couple of friends approaching. He looked forward to meeting them as their dog was a great friend of Billy's. Being distracted for less than a second he noticed that both figures had disappeared. On questioning his friends at their next meeting he learnt that they had not been in the vicinity that particular day.

Being in this area I found that some of my school memories were evoked. Some of the stretches of fields in the Embrook area were thought to be haunted by a lady cyclist. She was first reported by a lady walking her dog. I well remember how rumour became rife in those times – the finest imaginations of over 400 young boys were at their most active. The deluge was such that it obviously devalued any genuine incidents.

Finchampstead

In Finchampstead there is a strangely named house, the White Horse. This is not a pub, but a large and attractive manor house with spacious and charming gardens that are occasionally open to the public. Just to add to the confusion, there have been reports of a spectral white horse roaming the grounds of the manor. However, I believe this is a case of someone knowing someone that had seen it some time ago. Reports are unreliably scant to say the least.

Just a few hundred yards from the White Horse, near to the ancient village church, stands the Queen's Oak, the epitome of an English pub. There has long been reports here of a couple of spooks; an old lady who appeared at the bar, sometimes alone and sometimes accompanied by a small child, thought to be her grandson. In the early '90s stalwart regulars at the inn decided to put the old girl to rest with a séance. A group intent upon a mission and fortified by more accessible spirits sat around a table and endeavoured to communicate with those beyond.

I am not privy as to what exactly happened, but I am led to believe that they may have trodden a little further into the unknown than is conducive with peace of mind. Suffice to say that the more cynical among the party were somewhat less set in their skeptical opinions upon leaving. Incidentally, the old lady did not seem receptive.

'The Ghost That Never Was' (an article I wrote for the *Wokingham Times*) concerns a

The Queens Oak, Finchampstead.

house at the meeting of the Finchampstead and Lower Wokingham Road, very close to Gowrings Garage. In the 1960s, the house stood on its own and was left uninhabited for several years; youthful minds worked overtime. The building was nicknamed Cut Throat Cottage and stories were told of how a man had slit his wife's throat and then committed suicide by the same means. Quite incorrectly the rumour spread that the murderer could be witnessed at night bemoaning and bewailing his terrible deed.

However, I have traced every murder in Berkshire since 1720 and there certainly never was one in this particular vicinity. Let me offer a plausible explanation for this story. I discovered that this particular stretch of road at Handpost Corner is described on old maps as the Throat. The name obviously derives from the way the two roads resemble a human larynx – the rest is natural progression. The Throat became Cut Throat. and the house Cut

Old Forge, Finchampstead.

Throat Cottage. The murder, suicide and apparitions spawned of very vivid imaginations.

Now for a ghost story with some meat on it. It concerns a family that lived at the Old Forge at Finchampstead. The Forge was a shop when I knew it in the '60s. One of the ladies mentioned was still in residence and seemed to me to be a very levelheaded person indeed. The Old Forge was the venue for some of the most malicious and well-attested poltergeist activity ever reported. The trouble began in February 1926 and lasted until August of that year, by which time it had attracted nationwide acclaim and had been reported on the radio and by all the major national papers. At the time the Forge was inhabited by Mr Goswell, his wife and their two teenage daughters.

Firstly, a bath containing tins of nails and screws was turned over, followed swiftly by chairs doing somersaults, tables moving across floors and pictures flying from their hooks. Chests were turned upside down as were perambulators and bicycles. Bricks flew from solid walls – were replaced – then dropped out again. Bedclothes were ripped from beds, writing appeared on exercise books, walls and doors. Small objects were scattered everywhere. The word 'Go' appeared on the ceiling in the room which the whole family slept (for safety reasons). A pie was removed from a plate and was later discovered in a coal shed. A tin tray flew across the room and a cyclist passing by one day was nearly decapitated by a flying fireguard. A 10ft long carpenter's bench that took three men to move was effortlessly upended while the family slept.

The case did not escape the attention of the late Harry Price, prince amongst psychic investigators. The *Daily Mirror* did a daily report on the proceedings and over a dozen clairvoyants and investigators tried to exorcise the troubled spirit, but nothing could be done. The poltergeist activity ceased as quickly as it had begun in August 1926. I am reliably informed that there have been several minor hiccups since, but nothing resembling the 1926 activity.

During the activity at the Forge, Finchampstead possessed a very down to earth and cynical village constable. After inspecting the house one day and discovering nothing, he remonstrated with the family for wasting police time. As he turned to straddle his pedal cycle, a brick struck him on the shoulder.

Hurst

Hurst is sparsely populated and very widespread; it seems to the visitor that it has half a dozen small hamlets. The reason is said to be that in 1384, Hurst was stricken by the Black Death and to avoid contact with their neighbours people moved to the outskirts. This is possibly true, but why did this not happen to similar villages affected in the same way?

Hurst possesses several inns and reputedly the oldest bowling green in the country. Once known as the Church House, because it stands across the road from St Nicholas's, is the Castle Inn. The name seems somewhat strange, as there is not a castle in the vicinity.

The castle is reputed to have an underground passage to the church. It is also believed that bodies lay in state at the inn waiting their burial, while a carpenter constructed a coffin. This was called the Coffin Room; autopsies were commonly performed at inns.

There have been rumours of rumblings under the inn and ghostly moanings and also, there have been a couple of tragic deaths according to local legend. Firstly, in the 1800s a young serving girl who was playing silly games suffocated herself in a coffin – a story that has no doubt been well embroidered. Secondly, some fifty years later, a young boy dislodged a stack of coffins that crushed him to death. Though I do not doubt the poor child's demise, I suspect that villager's imaginations have been overactive on the cause. So there we have it; rumblings and mumblings from underground passages and cellars caused by the spirits of a young serving maid, a local schoolboy or possibly both.

Hurst Church.

The author at Hurst Pond.

Here is another piece of Hurst history: In the 1770s the village was home to an attractive young lady named Molly Tape. Friendly and helpful Molly was appreciated by the local wives for babysitting, shopping and other errands. Unfortunately, she was more than appreciated by the young men. Molly also had some questionable habits. It was once rumoured that, on the way to church, she wore a dress that exposed her ankles.

Molly fell in love with a local farmer, Dick Darvill, a man reputed to be a little fancy free where members of the opposite sex were concerned. Dick was eager to offer his advances to Molly and she was besotted by the handsome young farmer. They made a beautiful couple and planned to marry. They swore to each other to refrain from all others and to worship each other exclusively.

Molly was a lady of her word but Dick found temptation too much to handle.

Hearing of her betrothed's infidelity, Molly hanged herself from a beech tree in what came to be known as Tape Lane (incidentally there is also a Darvill's lane). But Molly's ghost was often witnessed, weeping, wailing and running in a distressed state around nearby Hurst Pond.

All seemed to be quiet for generations until Easter 1971, when Molly's ghost, this time seen in provocative underwear, was witnessed at the Pond. Several subsequent reports led to the story appearing in the local press. This in turn inevitably brought forth a series of jokers, scantily clad and adorned with long wigs, chasing around Hurst Pond in the moonlight. Finally a priest was called to exorcise poor Molly. The jokers found other amusements, the sightseers went home and peace descended on the village.

13

Sandhurst

SANDHURST is now described as a town, but to me and other locals it will always be a village. It is a long and snaking village that goes on for about 3 miles. On one of the bends near the western end is the Dukes Head, which is opposite the Rose and Crown.

New Road ran adjacent to the Dukes Head. My old granddad lived up there and owned a garage on the main road. Unfortunately, the close proximity of the two pubs was detrimental to his business and he never had sufficient funds to fill up the petrol tanks. For many years the Dukes Head, like most other small pubs, had a public bar and a saloon bar. The landlord was in a position to see who entered each bar simultaneously.

In the late 1970s, the landlord had friends staying with him. It was their habit to indulge in a mid-morning drink in the saloon bar. At this time of day things were generally quiet and the public bar was often deserted. On noticing a small man wearing a trilby in the mirror, the imbibers walked around to engage the local in conversation, but on reaching the public bar they found it deserted – and yet there was no exit other than the communal doorway in the hall between the two bars. It seems that the couple decided the occurrence

was strange but not worthy of mention to their friend, the landlord. However, the scene repeated itself the following day at the same time. There stood the little man complete with pint, black coat and trilby. This time they ran to the public bar but once again he had gone. They now decided to mention the two occurrences and the man's description to the landlord and a group of his regulars. All agreed that the description totally fitted a small imbibing regular who had frequented the inn but had died two years previously.

Heading east along the road to Camberley, we find Rackstraws, once Rack Straw Farm, now run by a group of restaurants and bars. Soon after the metamorphosis from farm to pub in the late 1960s, there was a large old oven here and a photo was taken to advertise it in a trade magazine. I knew the landlord but knew nothing of the photograph until we were chatting one day and it came up in conversation. He fetched it, and to my surprise there was a clearly defined skull pictured in the oven's recess. The skull was obviously genuine and one can be pretty sure the picture was.

In the 1960s they were not the opportunities for the photographic ingenuity that there is today. It would be a far more colourful

The Dukes Head, Sandhurst.

story if I had been able to discover a long lost murder at Rack Straw Farm, or at least an unsolved disappearance. Unfortunately I can trace neither event.

Broadmoor

There must be more than a thousand unusual stories about Broadmoor. However, very few are ghost stories. In fact there is only one and it's one that I have a tenuous association with.

In the 1960s and before, any suicide at Broadmoor went before a coroner and jury. Six good and honest men were hard to find in those days, especially in a small place like Crowthorne, where nearly everybody worked outside the village. I was working in my father's shop in those days and like other traders I was easy pickings. I remember one particular case very well. One poor inmate had hanged himself from a long upturned trestle table. It must have been a long and very painful death. Some of the photos we

were shown were horrific. We obviously brought a verdict of suicide and offered our condolences to the inmate's young son, then collected our expences (37.5 pence).

The reason I mention this case is that the unfortunate man is said to haunt one of the landings at Broadmoor. His spirit has been quite well attested to over the years and several male nurses have recounted strange experiences there. One in particular totally refused to go up there at night. Make of it what you will.

Owlsmoor

Once called Newfound Outland, it was started when builders and navvies, who worked on the construction of Broadmoor, married into families of gypsies who had settled nearby. In 1917, the first stories of a ghostly presence surfaced.

There is a bendy lane, now called South Road, that meanders from Broadmoor

Broadmoor Hospital.

Haunted Lavender Lane, leading off
South Road, Owlsmoor.

Hospital down to Owlsmoor. Midway, where the hospital property ends, there is a white gate that permanently prohibits motor transport advancing further south. There is a crossroads, or to be pedantic, cross paths; one leads back across Wildmoor Common to Crowthorne and the other, ironically named Lavender Lane, leads past the sewerage works to the Royal Military Academy at Sandhurst. It is near to this cross paths that an ancient female ghost has been witnessed on several occasions. The old crone is sometimes seen by herself and sometimes accompanied by a small child, usually assumed to be her granddaughter. Both seem to be of a benign nature.

There has been no fatal accident at or near the spot, so this couple is mysterious indeed. It is true that a large gypsy site was about 200 yards from the spot though. I knew all of the Romany gypsies there personally. All were aware of the pair of spooks, and usually their vivid imaginations would have conjured up a colourful story, but not this time.

Rack Straw Farm, Sandhurst.

14

Crowthorne

I have left my favourite story until the end. I was the first to discover it in a very old Reading newspaper.

In May 1883, a courting couple were walking in Crutchley Park. Crutchley Park was in the Sunninghill and Ascot area and is an extension of Broadmoor Woods, which in turn is part of the larger Bramshill Forest. The young couple were interrupted in their mutual appreciation by cries for help from somewhere among the trees. On inspection they found a middle-aged man stuck fast in the branches. After some considerable time the young man was able to liberate the pitiful prisoner. Once on firm ground he explained that his name was Henderson and he had been stuck in the tree for three days with no food and only tiny drops of rain water to drink. The thankful man was accompanied to Easthampstead Workhouse via the Crispin, where he could be forgiven for having acquired an ever capacious thirst. Having no visible means of support he was lodged at the Workhouse while his past was investigated. It seemed quite a mysterious past.

While Henderson was enjoying the hospitality of Easthampstead Workhouse for three days from 20 May to 23 May, he gave the police some information. He lived at Katesgrove Road in Reading. He was forty-nine years of age, a widower and lived with his two teenage daughters. He was a self-styled lay preacher with rather unusual interpretations of the Gospel. Eccentric to the extreme and described as menacingly ugly with a strong voice, he was a scary figure. It was his habit to climb on high buildings and trees and, using them as a substitute pulpit, he would preach fire and damnation to the adoring, if imaginary, congregation. Henderson signed himself out of the Workhouse early on 24 May after receiving a new set of clothes.

In October 1883, Robert Cole, a young forestry labourer was making his way through the dark foliage from Roundshill near Binfield to the Crowthorne Inn. It was twelve noon when he passed through an area known as Hagthorn, a deeply depressing area near the well-named Devil's Highway. There, Cole came across a badly decomposed body under a fallen tree. The young labourer sprinted to nearby Crowthorne where he gabbled his story to an acquaintance. They fetched a local constable who in turn fetched a wheelbarrow; the three then set off for Hagthorn.

Under the officer's instructions, the rotting body was transported to the Crowthorne Inn where it lay in state overnight, awaiting

The Devil's Highway, where Henderson's rotting corpse was discovered.

the scrutiny and investigating powers of Mr Weedon, the Bracknell coroner. One can imagine the landlord's reluctance – pubs were generally used for autopsies, but in this case the stench of putrefied flesh must have been abominable.

The remains were identified as James Henderson's. One witness, whose unenviable job it was to help with identification, was J.P. MacNillance, the superintendent at the Easthampstead Union Workhouse. MacNillance was able to identify a number stamped on the blue overalls that were allocated to Henderson in May.

The cause of Henderson's death will never be known. Mr Weedon stated that the remains were far too decomposed for even a general analysis. It could have been suicide,

murder or an accident – certainly not natural causes as Henderson was only forty-none and generally fit.

Incidentally, Hagthorn had witnessed two other suicides; one exactly fifty years before Henderson's demise. The body lay undiscovered for over a year, by which time there were only a few sodden strands left of the rope with which it was assumed the suicide victim hanged himself. This gave the Coroner's Court an insurmountable problem: could the atmosphere of these particular few acres provoke depression to the point of suicide? Naturally, Henderson – a grotesque, terrifying spectre haunts the area. Now where have I heard that before?

It was once possible to walk the 12 miles between Crowthorne and Windsor through the woods without crossing a tarmac road. Even today, there is only need to cross two, one of them being the A329 between Ascot and Virginia Water. Isn't this the road the phantom policeman walks – the one with the grossly deformed face? There are some remarkable similarities with Henderson here.

In the middle of the forestry where once stood a windmill, tales of the mean miller originated. After turning away the beggar who died on his doorstep, all went wrong for him. He starved to death in the Broadmoor Woods and his ghost has regularly been seen, reputedly a frighteningly ugly man.

Who was it that my friend Dooley saw when he was a child, living in a cottage at Caesar's Camp? He described him as a man with a terribly mutilated face. Could all of these spectres be Henderson?

A gentleman who worked at Broadmoor for decades told me a female cousin had come to visit him in the early 1970s. She was taking his dog for a walk in the forestry, when she saw something resembling a man emerge from the trees. He was scarily disfigured, with a persona that struck terror into her soul. Yet again, could this be Henderson?

Before leaving I feel bound to relate an episode that happened to a friend of mine in the 1960s. He was near the Broadmoor Reservoirs where his daughters, aged nine and seven, were enjoying a swim. Things were pretty basic in those days and the girls went to dry and dress behind the nearby laurel bushes. The next thing he knew, the girls came running out screaming, 'Daddy, Daddy a man!'

Thinking it to be some voyeur, my friend shot around the bushes, but there was no one to be seen and no way could anybody have moved fast enough to be out of sight. He returned to his daughters, who were genuinely distraught; there was no consoling them. When the panic finally abated he tried to ascertain a description.

The girls shouted in unison, 'It was an ogre, daddy, a terribly ugly ogre!' And that's where this terrifying encounter ends.

Other titles published by The History Press

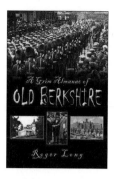

A Grim Almanac of Old Berkshire
ROGER LONG

A Grim Almanac of Old Berkshire is a day-by-day catalogue of ghastly tales dating fr
the twelfth to the twentieth centuries. It features the Watchfield farmer who tried
turn his wife into cooking fat, and the family who charged people to view their relati
decapitated body, as well as a plethora of poisonings, assaults, drownings, kidnappi
suicides and disasters. If you have ever wondered about what nasty goings-on occurred
the Berkshire of yesteryear, then look no further.

978 0 7524 5677 5

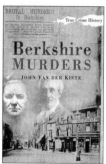

Berkshire Murders
JOHN VAN DER KISTE

Berkshire Murders reveals some of the county's most notorious and shocking cases, includ
that of Hannah Carey, beaten to death by her husband at Warfield in 1851; Nell Woodric
murdered by her husband in 1896 and later immortalised in Oscar Wilde's 'The Ballad
Reading Gaol'; and Minnie Freeman Lee, whose body was discovered in a trunk in 19
John Van der Kiste's well-illustrated and enthralling text will appeal to all those interes
in the darker side of Berkshire's history.

978 0 7509 5129 6

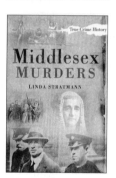

Middlesex Murders
LINDA STRATMANN

Middlesex Murders brings together numerous murderous tales, some of which made natio
headlines. They include the murder of John Draper, whose body was found in a well
Enfield Chase in 1816; fifteen-year-old John Brill, found beaten to death in a wood
1837 after giving evidence against two poachers; and Claire Paul, killed with an axe at I
home in Ruislip in 1938. Linda Stratmann's carefully researched and gripping text v
appeal to everyone interested in the shady side of Middlesex's history.

978 0 7524 5123 7

1970s London: Discovering the Capital
ALEC FORSHAW

Following a sheltered childhood, Alec Forshaw was ready for a dose of the wider wor
London in the early 1970s was where the lights shone brightest. But it was also a city f
of declining industries and derelict docklands, a townscape blighted by undeveloped bor
sites, demonic motorway proposals and slum clearance schemes. This sequel to *Growing*
in Cambridge portrays the London of over thirty years ago as it appeared to a young ma
stumbling across the sights and sounds of an extraordinary city.

978 0 7524 5691 1

Visit our website and discover thousands of other History Press books.
www.thehistorypress.co.uk